I0491245

TRANSPORTATION ECONOMIC TRENDS

U.S. Department of Transportation
Bureau of Transportation Statistics

ACKNOWLEDGEMENTS

U.S. Department of Transportation

Anthony Foxx
Secretary of Transportation

Victor Mendez
Deputy Secretary of Transportation

Gregory Winfree
Assistant Secretary for Research and Technology

Bureau of Transportation Statistics

Patricia Hu
Director

Rolf Schmitt
Deputy Director

Produced under the direction of:
Karen E. White
Director, Office of Statistical and Economic Analysis

Major Contributors
Stephen Brumbaugh
Kenneth Notis

Other Contributors
Edward Ross Crichton
Bernetta Crutcher
Theresa Firestine
David Smallen
Sonya Smith
Connie Tang

Editor
William H. Moore

Visual Information Specialist
Alpha Wingfield

QUALITY ASSURANCE STATEMENT

The Bureau of Transportation Statistics (BTS) provides high quality information to serve government, industry, and the public in a manner that promotes broad understanding. Standards and policies are used to ensure and maximize the quality, objectivity, utility and integrity of its information. BTS reviews quality issues on a regular basis and adjusts its programs and processes to ensure continuous quality improvement.

Notice

This document is disseminated under the sponsorship of the U.S. Department of Transportation in the interest of information exchange. The U.S. Government assumes no liability for its contents or use thereof.

ABOUT THIS REPORT

Transportation plays a vital role in the American economy: it makes economic activity possible, and serves as a major economic activity in its own right.

This report is BTS's first stand-alone volume on transportation and the economy, and uses a variety of data series to highlight relevant trends and explain related measurement concepts. The report has eight chapters:

- Chapter 1 introduces the Transportation Services Index, a monthly summary of freight and passenger movement.

- Chapter 2 explains what transportation contributes to the American economy.

- Chapter 3 examines the costs that households and businesses pay for transportation.

- Chapter 4 analyzes transportation-related employment.

- Chapter 5 explains and examines trends in transportation productivity.

- Chapter 6 analyzes household spending on transportation goods and services.

- Chapter 7 examines government transportation spending and revenue.

- Chapter 8 discusses the value of transportation.

Each chapter uses the latest data available at the time of publication.

TABLE OF CONTENTS

1 SUMMARY INDICATORS

Introduction to Summary Indicators

Transportation is a service industry, moving people and goods for the benefit of businesses and households. Whether it is a vacation trip, a shipment of raw inputs to a manufacturer, or final product delivery to a consumer, transportation services are a key barometer of economic activity.

The U.S. Department of Transportation's (DOT) Bureau of Transportation Statistics (BTS) developed and currently produces the Transportation Services Index (TSI) to measure the volume of services provided monthly by the for-hire transportation sector (box 1-1).[1]

---

[1]For-hire transportation consists of the services provided by transportation firms to industries and the public on a fee basis. Airlines, railroads, transit agencies, common carrier trucking companies, and pipelines are examples of for-hire transportation. Other types of transportation are discussed in Chapter 2 in the context of the Transportation Satellite Accounts.

Box 1-1 Transportation Services Index

The Transportation Services Index (TSI), produced by the U.S. Department of Transportation, Bureau of Transportation Statistics (BTS), measures the movement of freight and passengers. The Bureau produces three indexes—a freight index, a passenger index, and a total or combined index. The indexes combine monthly data from multiple for-hire transportation modes. Each index shows the month-to-month change in for-hire transportation services. Monthly data on each mode of transportation is seasonally adjusted and then combined into the three indexes. The passenger index is a weighted average of data for passenger aviation, transit, and passenger rail. The freight index is a weighted average of data for trucking, freight rail, waterborne, pipeline, and air freight. The combined index is a weighted average of all these modes. These indexes serve both as multimodal monthly measures of the state of transportation, and as indicators of the U.S. economic future.

SOURCE: Bureau of Transportation Statistics, 2016.

Transportation Services Index

Figure 1-1 shows the steps used to create the TSI, from collecting raw data, through seasonally adjusting and indexing the data, to combining

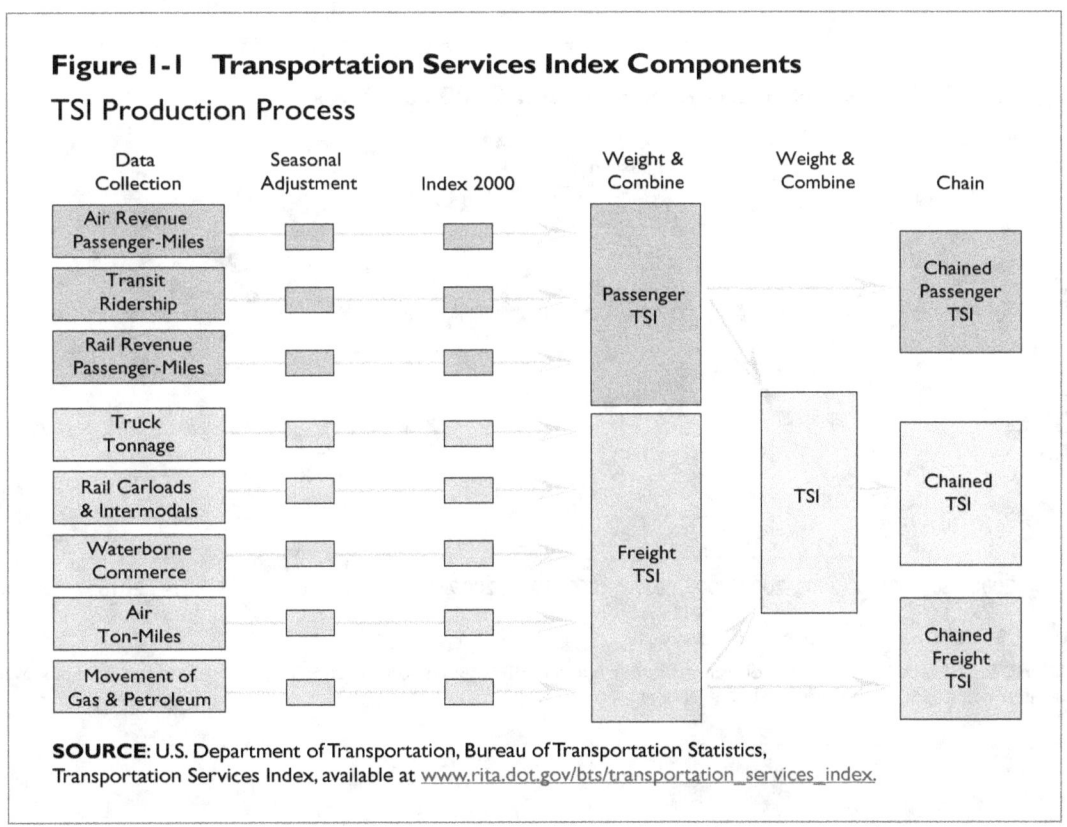

Figure 1-1 Transportation Services Index Components
TSI Production Process

SOURCE: U.S. Department of Transportation, Bureau of Transportation Statistics, Transportation Services Index, available at www.rita.dot.gov/bts/transportation_services_index.

them into summary chained indexes (box 1-2). The green boxes in figure 1-1 highlight the data input and process for the passenger TSI, while the blue boxes highlight the data input and process for the freight TSI. The two indexes are then appropriately weighted to create the combined TSI.

Figure 1-2 illustrates trends in the TSI from January 2000 to March 2016. Overall, the combined TSI increased by 19.0 percent, the freight TSI increased by 13.9 percent, and the passenger TSI increased by 30.9 percent. However, all three measures declined in the wake of the September 2001 terrorist attacks. The passenger TSI dropped especially sharply—19.3 percent from August 2001 to September 2001. All three indexes also decreased sharply during the recession from December 2007 to June 2009. The combined TSI decreased by 19.3 percent, the passenger TSI decreased by 6.6 percent, and the freight TSI decreased by 11.4 percent. However, they have all since recovered to prerecession levels.

TSI and the Economy

The TSI has a strong relationship with the economy, and the TSI has increased as the

---

Box 1-2 Chained Indexing

Many economic measures use a fixed base year to allow comparisons over time. However, the measures are highly sensitive to the base year chosen, and choosing a new base year can change the measure's history dramatically. In the past, when government economists changed the base year for calculating GDP, the revised growth calculations sparked numerous debates about the true state of the economy. At the same time, however, these measures become less accurate the further one moves away from the base year due to an effect known as "substitution bias." In other words, keeping the base year fixed introduces a new problem.

One method to address these issues is chaining, a technique that uses values from the current year and the fixed year to calculate values. Chaining is more computationally difficult, but more accurate because it can account for substitution bias. For the Transportation Services Index, the Bureau of Transportation Services uses the Fisher Ideal Index formula to chain the data. Technical details are available at http://1.usa.gov/1PWbN8T.

SOURCE: Bureau of Transportation Statistics, 2016.

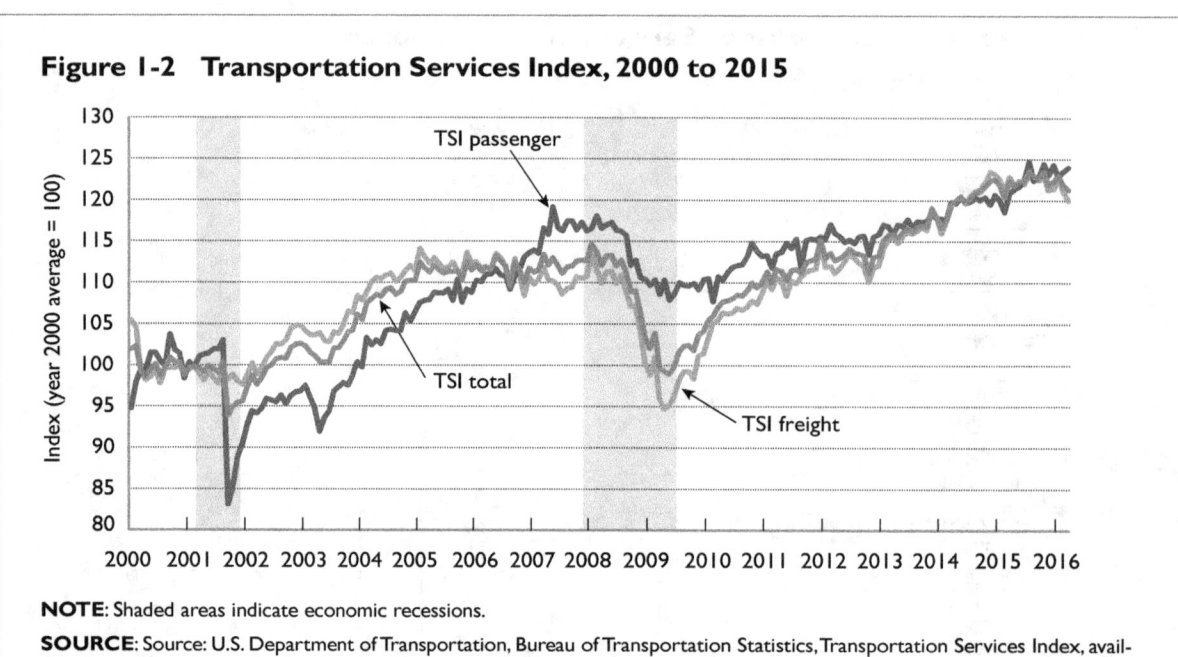

Figure 1-2 Transportation Services Index, 2000 to 2015

NOTE: Shaded areas indicate economic recessions.

SOURCE: Source: U.S. Department of Transportation, Bureau of Transportation Statistics, Transportation Services Index, available at www.rita.dot.gov/bts/transportation_services_index.

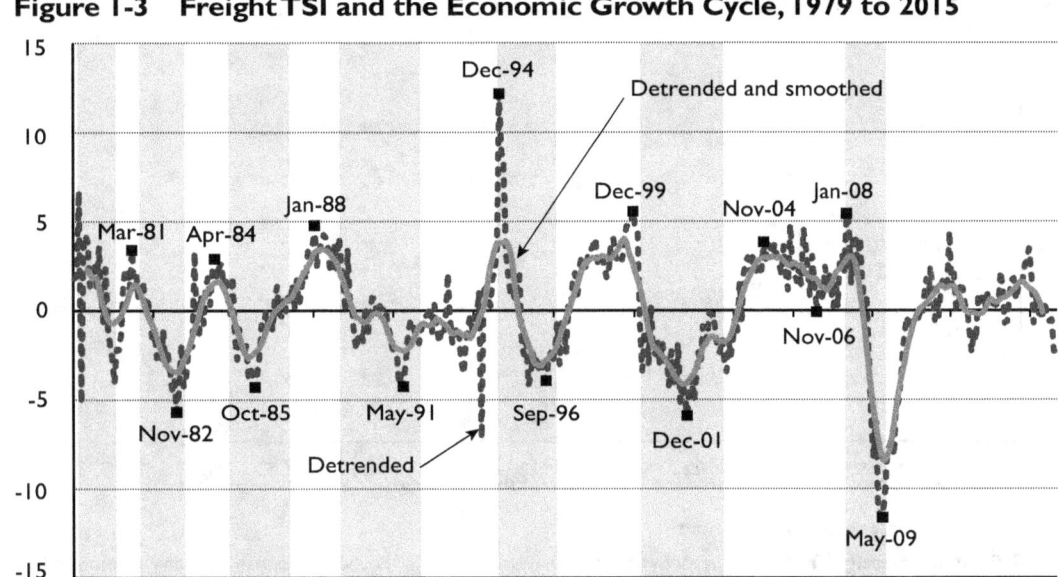

Figure 1-3 Freight TSI and the Economic Growth Cycle, 1979 to 2015

NOTES: Shaded areas indicate decelerations in the economy (growth cycles). Detrending and smoothing refer to statistical procedures that make it easier to observe changes in upturns and downturns of the data. Detrending removes the long-term growth trend and smoothing eliminates month-to-month volatility.

SOURCE: U.S. Department of Transportation, Bureau of Transportation Statistics, Transportation Services Index, available at www.bts.gov as of May 2016.

economy has grown. BTS research shows that changes in the TSI occur before changes in the economy, making the TSI useful for predicting economic trends.[2] Figure 1-3 illustrates the relationship between the freight TSI and the national economy from 1979 to 2015. The dashed blue line shows the freight TSI detrended to remove long-term changes. The red line shows the freight TSI detrended and smoothed to eliminate month-to-month volatility as well. The shaded areas represent *economic slowdowns*, or periods when economic growth slows below normal rates and unemployment rises as a result. The peaks and troughs marked in figure 1-3 show that the freight TSI usually peaks before a growth slowdown begins and hits a trough before a growth slowdown ends.

---

2 See U.S. Department of Transportation, Bureau of Transportation Statistics, *TSI and the Economy Revisited*, December 2014, available at www.rita.dot.gov/bts/sites/rita.dot.gov.bts/files/publications/special_reports_and_issue_briefs/special_report/2014_12_10/html/entire.html

To understand the relationships between transportation and the rest of the economy, one can compare trends in the TSI with trends in other economic measures. The economic measures are presented as indexes for comparability with the TSI.

Gross Domestic Product (GDP) and Foreign Trade

Gross Domestic Product (GDP) is the broadest measure of the economy. The U.S. GDP includes the monetary value of all goods and services produced within the United States. Between the first quarters of 2000 and 2016, real GDP increased 33.4 percent, and the freight TSI increased by 17.8 percent (figure 1-4). However, due to the recession, GDP decreased 3.6 percent from the first quarter of 2008 to the second quarter of 2009, and the freight TSI decreased 14.6 percent. Both measures have since recovered to prerecession levels. GDP includes

3

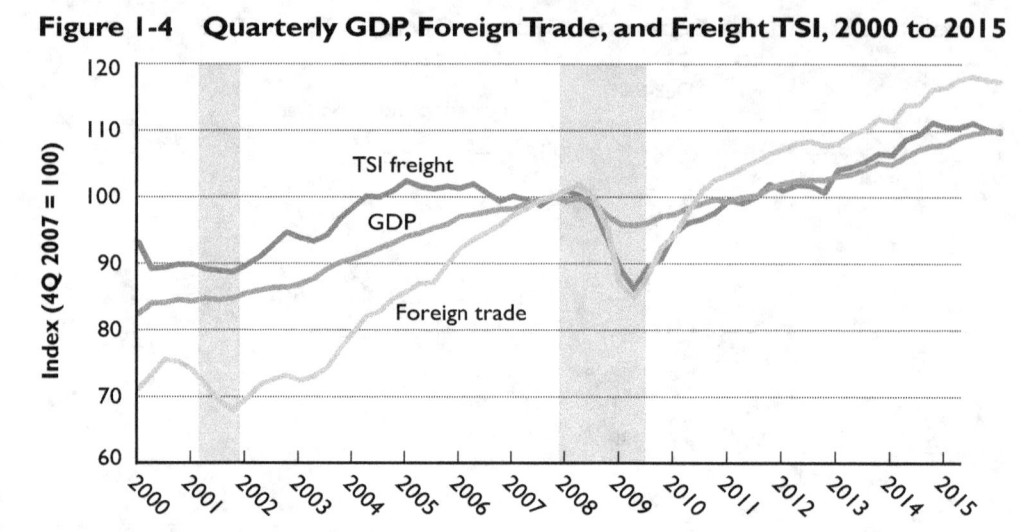

Figure 1-4 Quarterly GDP, Foreign Trade, and Freight TSI, 2000 to 2015

NOTE: Shaded areas indicate economic recessions.

SOURCES: **GDP and Foreign Trade**: U.S. Department of Commerce, Bureau of Economic Analysis, National Income and Product Accounts, table 1.1.6, available at www.bea.gov/iTable/index_nipa.cfm. Foreign trade is the sum of imports and exports. **Freight TSI**: U.S. Department of Transportation, Bureau of Transportation Statistics, Transportation Services Index, available at www.rita.dot.gov/bts/transportation_services_index.

many sectors besides transportation, so the magnitude of changes in GDP and the TSI cannot be directly compared.

In addition to domestic value shown by GDP, figure 1-4 includes the real foreign trade index to capture import and export activity. Real foreign trade increased 64.9 percent between the first quarters of 2000 and 2016, outpacing GDP growth. During the recession, foreign trade declined 15.9 percent from the first quarter of 2008 to the second quarter of 2009.

Industrial Production and Manufacturers' Shipments

Industrial production and manufacturers' shipments are major sources of demand for freight transportation services (box 1-3). When these shipments declined during the recession, the freight TSI declined as well (figure 1-5). From December 2007 to July 2009, industrial production declined by 16 percent, and

Box 1-3   Industrial Production and Manufacturers' Shipments

The Industrial Production Index is published monthly by the Federal Reserve Board and measures real output in the U.S. industrial sector, which includes manufacturing, mining, and electric and gas utilities.

Data on manufacturers' shipments come from the Census Bureau's Manufacturers' Shipments, Inventories, and Orders (M3) survey, which provides monthly data on economic conditions in the domestic manufacturing sector. The survey measures the dollar value of products sold by manufacturing establishments and is based on net selling values after discounts and allowances are excluded. Freight charges and excise taxes are also excluded.

SOURCE: Bureau of Transportation Statistics, 2016.

manufacturers' shipments declined by 21 percent. After the recession, industrial production increased by 17 percent, and manufacturers' shipments increased by 28 percent. However, manufacturers' shipments recently declined 8.6 percent from July 2014 to March 2016.

4

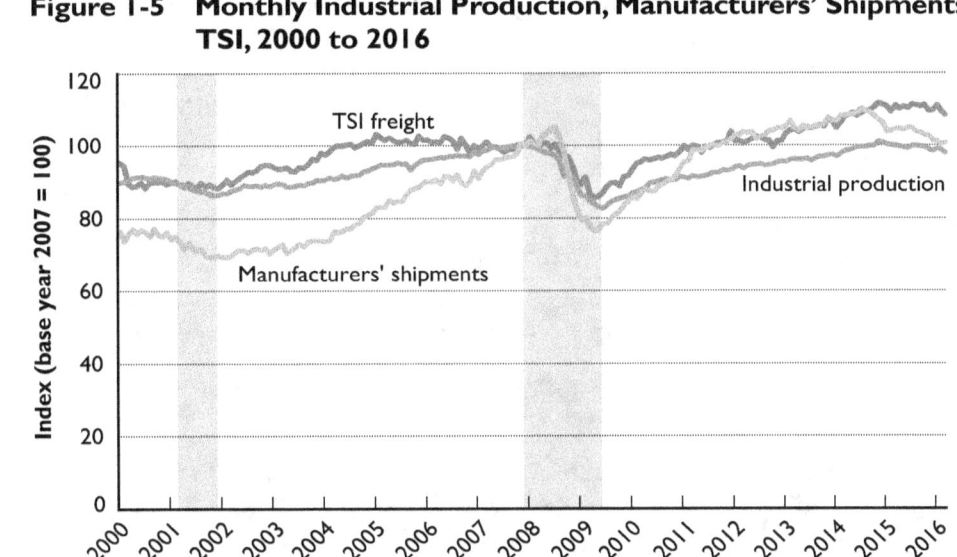

Figure 1-5 Monthly Industrial Production, Manufacturers' Shipments, and Freight TSI, 2000 to 2016

NOTE: Shaded areas indicate economic recessions.

SOURCES: Industrial Production: Board of Governors of the Federal Reserve System (US), *Industrial Production Index* [IN-DPRO], retrieved from FRED, Federal Reserve Bank of St. Louis https://research.stlouisfed.org/fred2/series/INDPRO/, May 2016.
Manufacturers' Shipments: US Bureau of the Census, *Value of Manufacturers' Shipments for All Manufacturing Industries* [AMT-MVS], retrieved from FRED, Federal Reserve Bank of St. Louis https://research.stlouisfed.org/fred2/series/AMTMVS/, May 2016.
Freight TSI: U.S. Department of Transportation, Bureau of Transportation Statistics, Transportation Services Index, available at www.rita.dot.gov/bts/transportation_services_index.

Inventories/Sales Ratio

When businesses keep greater amounts of inventory on hand, they use less freight transportation. One measure of inventory on hand is the *inventories/sales ratio*, or the value of goods on shelves and warehouses divided by monthly sales. A ratio of 2.5, for example, would indicate that a business has enough goods to cover sales for 2.5 months. When the inventories/sales ratio rises, the freight TSI declines at the same time or soon after. Conversely, when businesses move greater amounts of inventory and inventories/sales ratio falls, the freight TSI increases.

The U.S. Census Bureau produces a national inventories/sales ratio for businesses in the United States. This ratio has generally declined as businesses adopt just-in-time delivery and learn to manage their inventory more efficiently. From January 2000 to June 2008, the ratio declined by about 9 percent from 1.38 to 1.25 (figure 1-6). During the recession, however, the ratio rose to 1.48 in January 2009—an increase of 18 percent in less than a year. Correspondingly, the freight TSI declined 10.1 percent from June 2008 to January 2009.

Seasonally Adjusted Transportation Data

The monthly data used to create the TSI are highly seasonal, reflecting trends such as stores increasing inventory for the holiday season and households taking vacations in the summer. Seasonal trends make it difficult to observe underlying long-term changes in the data, as well as monthly shifts and short term trends, which are best viewed using seasonally adjusted data (box 1-4).

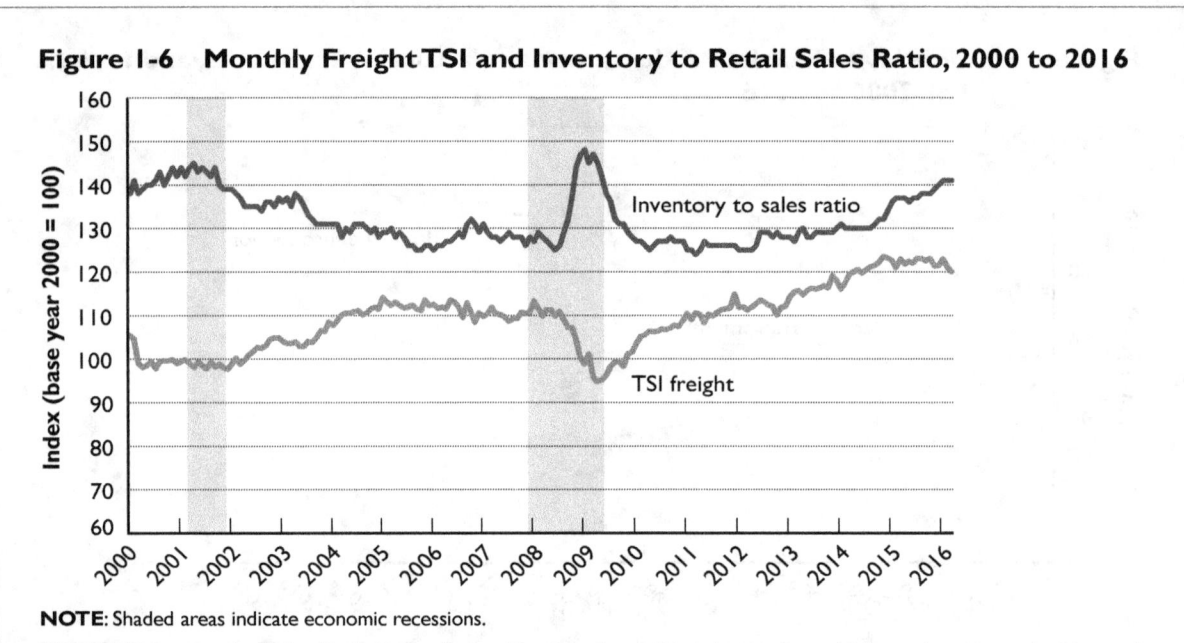

Figure 1-6   Monthly Freight TSI and Inventory to Retail Sales Ratio, 2000 to 2016

NOTE: Shaded areas indicate economic recessions.

SOURCES: **Inventories/Sales Ratio**: Census Bureau, Manufacturing and Trade Inventories and Sales, www.census.gov/mtis/.
Freight TSI: U.S. Department of Transportation, Bureau of Transportation Statistics, Transportation Services Index, available at www.rita.dot.gov/bts/transportation_services_index.

Box 1-4   Seasonal Adjustment

Seasonal adjustment is the process of estimating and removing seasonal movement. Seasonal adjustment decomposes a time series into a seasonal part and an irregular part. The goal is to remove changes in the data happening at the same time and with the same magnitude and direction every year. Controlling these predictable influences allows measurement of real monthly changes, short and long term patterns of growth or decline and turning points.

SOURCE: Bureau of Transportation Statistics, 2016.

To portray real changes in the TSI, BTS seasonally adjusts, indexes, and weights the data based on economic value added[3] for all transportation modes including truck tonnage, rail freight carloads, rail freight intermodal, pipeline, natural gas, U.S. waterway tonnage, passenger air transportation, rail passenger-miles, and public transit ridership. Figures 1-7 through 1-17 show the raw and seasonally adjusted data for each of

the modes included in the TSI, except for truck tonnage, which shows only the seasonally adjusted data.[4]

Seasonally Adjusted Freight Transportation

Seasonally adjusted truck tonnage increased by 25.4 percent between January 2000 and March 2016 (figure 1-7). After reaching a recession-related low in April 2009, the index has increased by 35.1 percent.

Seasonally adjusted rail carloads decreased by 26.1 percent from January 2000 to March 2016 (figure 1-8). Carloads declined by the greatest amount during the 2007 to 2009 recession, and never recovered to prerecession levels. Moreover, carloads began to decline again in December 2014. In March 2016 carloads dropped to 1.05 million— the lowest amount in the last 16 years, and the

---

[3] Value added is defined as industry gross output less purchased materials and purchased services. This is a measure of the size of an industry sector used by economists. Value added for all industries sums to Gross Domestic Product.

[4] Seasonally adjusted truck tonnage - is calculated from the American Trucking Association Monthly Truck Tonnage Report. For unadjusted truck tonnage data, contact the American Trucking Association.

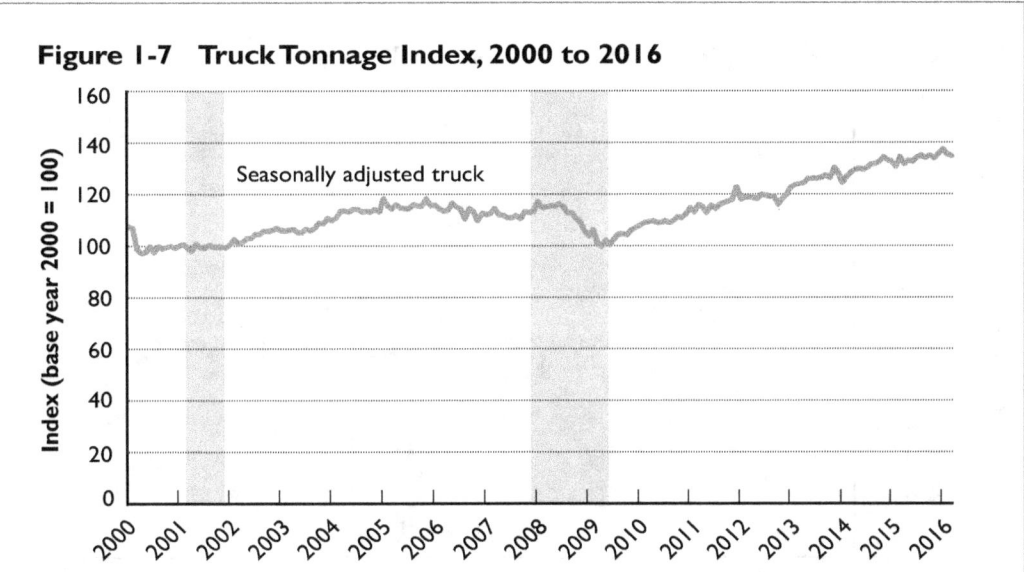

Figure 1-7   Truck Tonnage Index, 2000 to 2016

NOTES: Shaded areas indicate economic recessions. The unadjusted truck tonnage data are available from the American Trucking Association's (ATA) Monthly Truck Tonnage Report. Under agreement with the ATA, BTS does not publish the unadjusted series.

SOURCES: U.S. Department of Transportation, Bureau of Transportation Statistics, seasonally adjusted transportation data, available at www.transtats.bts.gov/osea/seasonaladjustment/, as of May 2016.

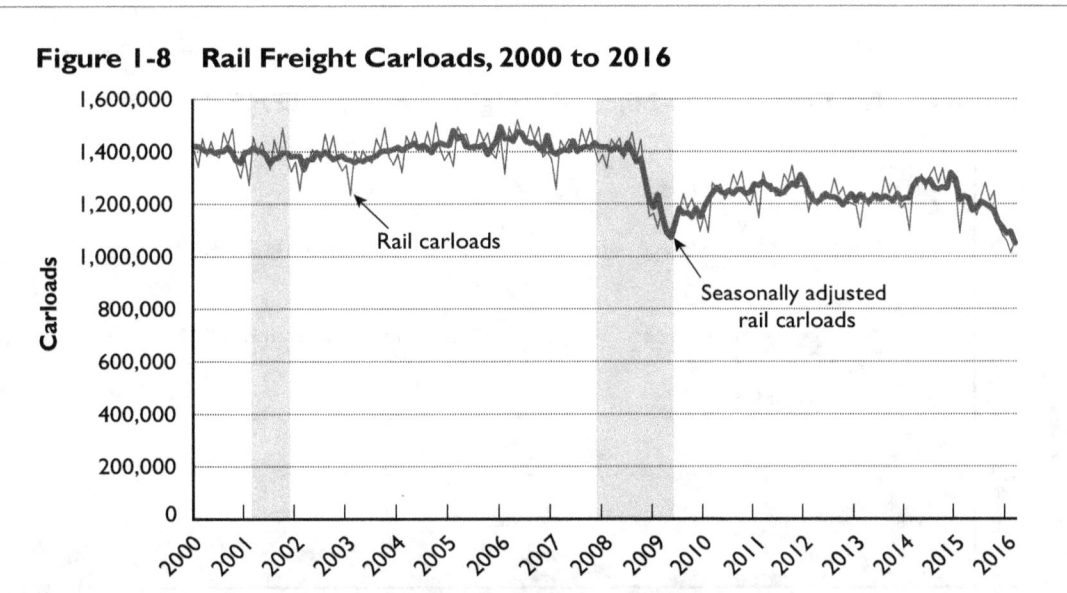

Figure 1-8   Rail Freight Carloads, 2000 to 2016

NOTES: Shaded areas indicate economic recessions. Monthly rail carloads and intermodals are estimated by dividing the weekly sum by 7 (7 days in a week) and then summing for the number of days in the month (31 days for May, 30 days for June, etc.).

SOURCES: U.S. Department of Transportation, Bureau of Transportation Statistics, seasonally adjusted transportation data, available at www.transtats.bts.gov/osea/seasonaladjustment/, as of May 2016. Rail freight carloads - Association of American Railroads and available through Railfax: railfax.transmatch.com/.

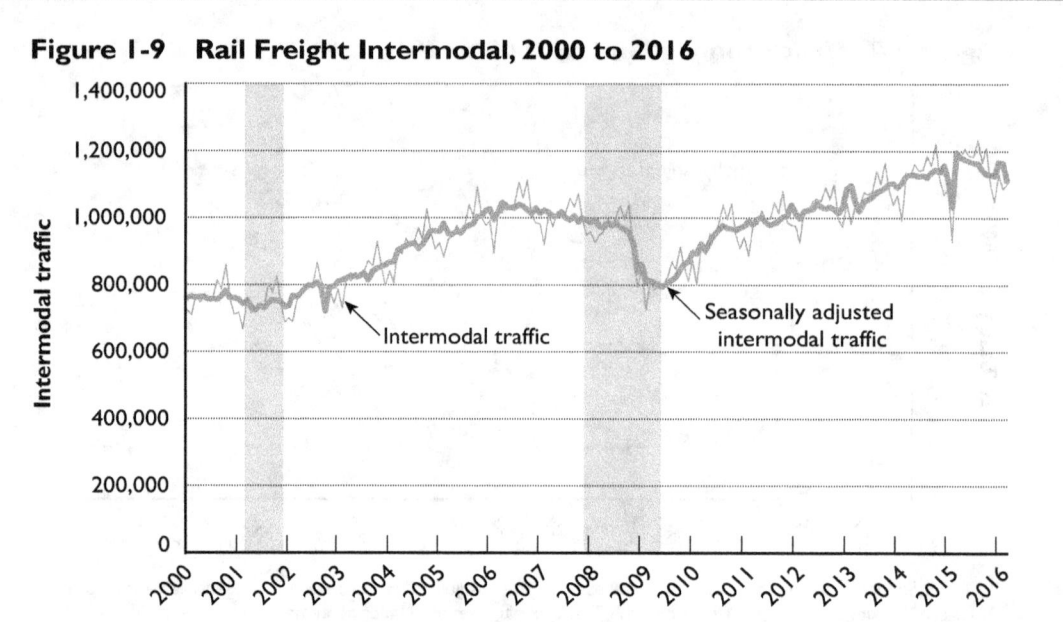

Figure 1-9   Rail Freight Intermodal, 2000 to 2016

Intermodal traffic

Seasonally adjusted
intermodal traffic

NOTES: Shaded areas indicate economic recessions. Monthly rail carloads and intermodals are estimated by dividing the weekly sum by 7 (7 days in a week) and then summing for the number of days in the month.

SOURCES: U.S. Department of Transportation, Bureau of Transportation Statistics, seasonally adjusted transportation data, available at www.transtats.bts.gov/osea/seasonaladjustment/, as of May 2016. Rail freight intermodal traffic - Association of American Railroads and available through Railfax: railfax.transmatch.com/.

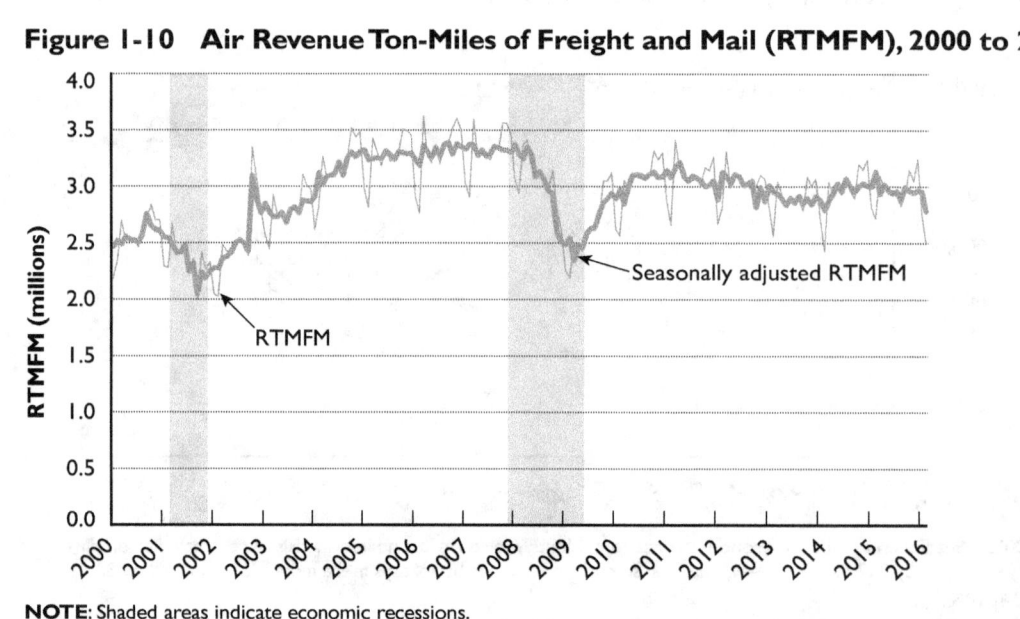

Figure 1-10   Air Revenue Ton-Miles of Freight and Mail (RTMFM), 2000 to 2016

Seasonally adjusted RTMFM

RTMFM

NOTE: Shaded areas indicate economic recessions.

SOURCES: U.S. Department of Transportation, Bureau of Transportation Statistics, seasonally adjusted transportation data, available at www.transtats.bts.gov/osea/seasonaladjustment/, as of May 2016.
Unadjusted RTMFM - U.S. Department of Transportation, Bureau of Transportation Statistics (BTS), Office of Airline Information, T-1 data Seasonally adjusted RTMFM - U.S. Department of Transportation, Bureau of Transportation Statistics (BTS).

first time that carloads have dropped below the recession-era low of May 2009. Rail carloads have declined in large part because demand for coal, the main freight railroad commodity, has decreased. In 2014 Class I railroads originated 18.8 percent fewer tons of coal than in 2008.[5]

In contrast to rail carloads, seasonally adjusted rail intermodal traffic has increased by 46.0 percent from January 2000 to March 2016 (figure 1-9). It has increased by 39.6 percent from its recession-era low in June 2009, which was still higher than its level in January 2000.

Seasonally adjusted aviation freight ton-miles have increased by 13.1 percent in the last 16 years and by 19.0 percent since their recession-era low in March 2009 but have still not returned to their pre-recession levels (figure 1-10).

_____

[5] See Association of American Railroads, "Railroads and Coal," July 2015, available at www.aar.org/BackgroundPapers/Railroads%20and%20Coal.pdf.

Seasonally adjusted waterway tonnage declined by 13.4 percent from January 2000 to March 2016. It has recovered by 41.3 percent since its low in October 2009, though its March 2016 level is below the high it reached in later 2014 (figure 1-11).

Seasonally adjusted petroleum pipeline shipments increased from 212 million barrels of crude oil in January 2000 to 248 million barrels in March 2016, fueled largely by an increase in shipments from August 2014 to the present (figure 1-12). Unlike other transportation measures, which declined noticeably during the 2007 to 2009 recession, pipeline shipments declined steadily over a longer period from late 2004 to late 2009.

Seasonally adjusted natural gas consumption, which measures transportation of natural gas by pipeline, has increased by 17.9 percent since 2000 and is highly seasonal (figure 1-13).

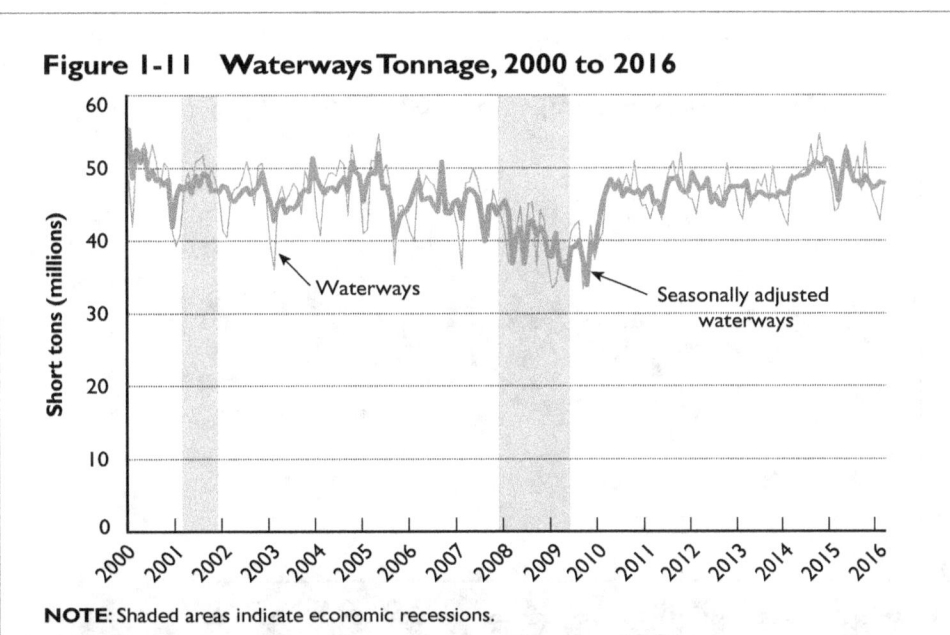

Figure 1-11 Waterways Tonnage, 2000 to 2016

NOTE: Shaded areas indicate economic recessions.

SOURCES: U.S. Department of Transportation, Bureau of Transportation Statistics, seasonally adjusted transportation data, available at www.transtats.bts.gov/osea/seasonaladjustment/, as of May 2016.
Tonnage carried on internal U.S. waterways - U.S. Army Corps of Engineers, Waterborne Commerce Statistics Center, Internal U.S. Waterway Monthly Tonnage Indicators available at www.navigationdatacenter.us/wcsc/wcmthind.htm.
Seasonally-adjusted tonnage carried on internal U.S. waterways - U.S. Department of Transportation, Bureau of Transportation Statistics (BTS) calculation from U.S. Army Corps of Engineers, Waterborne Commerce Statistics Center, Internal U.S. Waterway Monthly Tonnage Indicators available at www.navigationdatacenter.us/wcsc/wcmthind.htm.

Figure 1-12 Pipeline Petroleum, 2000 to 2016

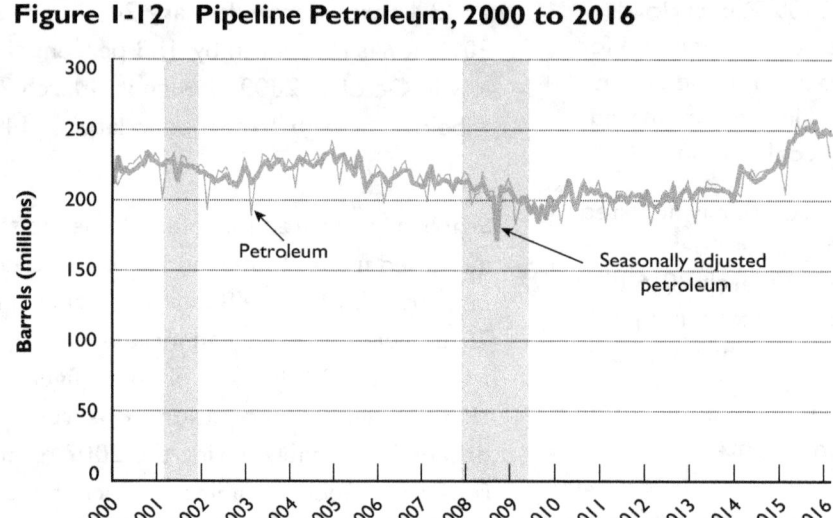

NOTE: Shaded areas indicate economic recessions.

SOURCES: U.S. Department of Transportation, Bureau of Transportation Statistics, seasonally adjusted transportation data, available at www.transtats.bts.gov/osea/seasonaladjustment/, as of May 2016. Pipeline movement - U.S. Energy Information Administration (EIA) available at: www.eia.gov/petroleum/supply/monthly/ (Table 58); tonto.eia.doe.gov/dnav/pet/pet_crd_crpdn_adc_mbbl_m.htm (Alaska) Seasonally-adjusted pipeline movement - U.S. Department of Transportation, Bureau of Transportation Statistics (BTS) calculation from data collected by U.S. Energy Information Administration (EIA) available at: www.eia.gov/petroleum/supply/monthly/ (Table 58); tonto.eia.doe.gov/dnav/pet/pet_crd_crpdn_adc_mbbl_m.htm (Alaska).

Figure 1-13 Natural Gas Consumption, 2000 to 2016

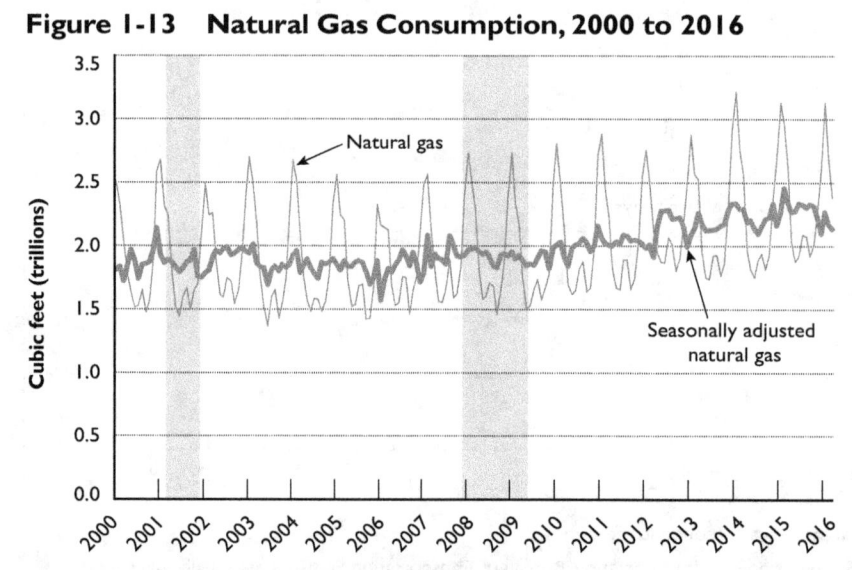

NOTE: Shaded areas indicate economic recessions.

SOURCES: U.S. Department of Transportation, Bureau of Transportation Statistics, seasonally adjusted transportation data, available at www.transtats.bts.gov/osea/seasonaladjustment/, as of May 2016. Natural gas consumption - U.S. Energy Information Administration (EIA) available at: www.eia.gov/dnav/ng/hist/n9140us2m.htm; www.eia.doe.gov/emeu/steo/pub/contents.html (forecast). Seasonally-adjusted natural gas consumption - U.S. Department of Transportation, Bureau of Transportation Statistics (BTS) calculation from data collected by U.S. Energy Information Administration (EIA) available at: www.eia.gov/dnav/ng/hist/n9140us2m.htm; www.eia.doe.gov/emeu/steo/pub/contents.html (forecast).

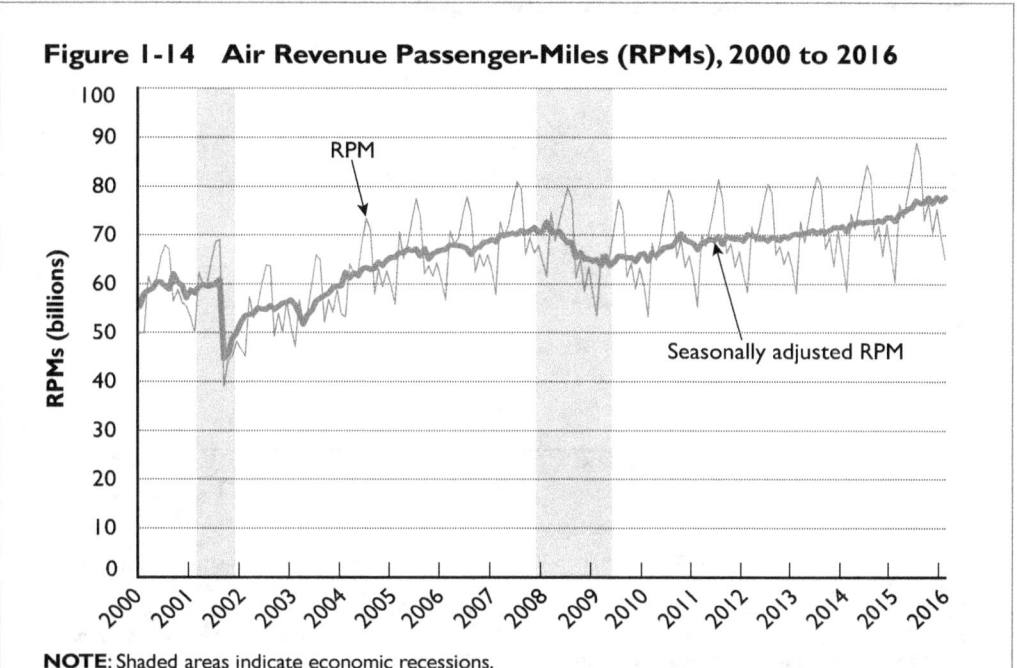

Figure 1-14 Air Revenue Passenger-Miles (RPMs), 2000 to 2016

RPM

Seasonally adjusted RPM

RPMs (billions)

NOTE: Shaded areas indicate economic recessions.

SOURCES: U.S. Department of Transportation, Bureau of Transportation Statistics, seasonally adjusted transportation data, available at www.transtats.bts.gov/osea/seasonaladjustment/, as of May 2016. Unadjusted RPMs - U.S. Department of Transportation, Bureau of Transportation Statistics (BTS), Office of Airline Information, T-1 data. Seasonally adjusted RPMs - U.S. Department of Transportation, Bureau of Transportation Statistics (BTS).

Seasonally Adjusted Passenger Transportation

Seasonally adjusted air passenger-miles have increased by 40.9 percent in the last 16 years (figure 1-14). They reached their lowest point in September 2001 following the 9/11 terrorist attacks, but have increased by 74.0 percent since that point.

Seasonally adjusted transit ridership has increased by 10.2 percent in the last 16 years, but has not yet recovered to the high points reached in July 2008, just before the recession, and the even earlier May 2007 peak (figure 1-15).

Seasonally adjusted rail passenger-miles have increased by 21.3 percent since 2000. They reached their highest level in April 2012 (figure 1-16).

While the TSI measures for-hire transportation services, BTS also seasonally adjusts data for highway vehicle-miles traveled (VMT) to show trends in travel volumes. Seasonally adjusted VMT has grown by 16.7 percent since January 2000 (figure 1-17).

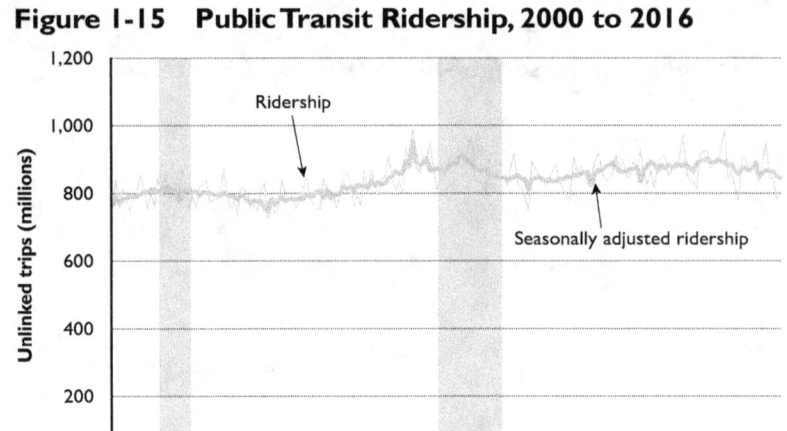

Figure 1-15   Public Transit Ridership, 2000 to 2016

NOTE: Shaded areas indicate economic recessions.

SOURCES: U.S. Department of Transportation, Bureau of Transportation Statistics, seasonally adjusted transportation data, available at www.transtats.bts.gov/osea/seasonaladjustment/, as of May 2016. Public transit ridership - American Public Transportation Association (APTA) data (2000 through 2009) available at: www.apta.com/resources/statistics/Pages/ridershipreport.aspx and U.S. Department of Transportation, Federal Transit Administration, National Transit Database (2010 to present) available at: www.ntdprogram.gov/ntdprogram/data.htm Seasonally-adjusted public transit ridership - U.S. Department of Transportation, Bureau of Transportation Statistics (BTS) calculation from American Public Transportation Association (APTA) data (2000 through 2009) available at: www.apta.com/resources/statistics/Pages/ridershipreport.aspx and U.S. Department of Transportation, Federal Transit Administration, National Transit Database (2010 to present) available at: www.ntdprogram.gov/ntdprogram/data.htm.

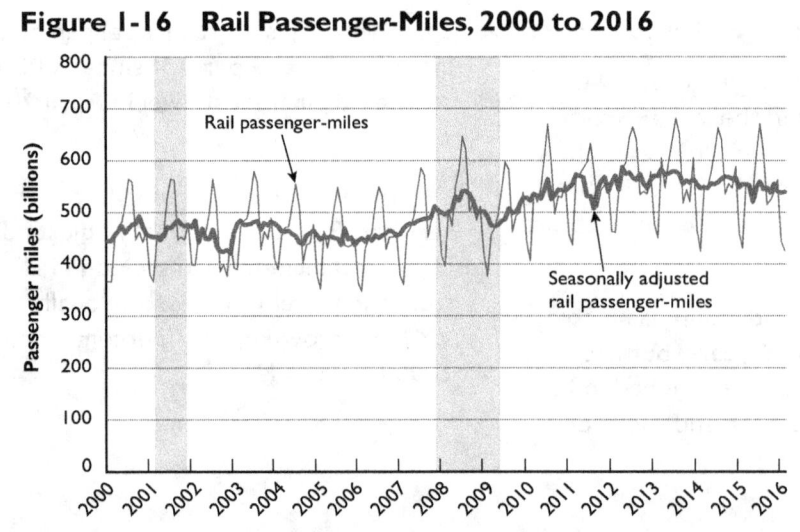

Figure 1-16   Rail Passenger-Miles, 2000 to 2016

NOTES: Shaded areas indicate economic recessions. "Rail" includes Amtrak and Alaska Railroad Corporation, but not commuter rail.

SOURCES: U.S. Department of Transportation, Bureau of Transportation Statistics, seasonally adjusted transportation data, available at www.transtats.bts.gov/osea/seasonaladjustment/ as of May 2016. Rail passenger miles - U.S. Department of Transportation, Federal Railroad Administration available at: safety-data.fra.dot.gov/OfficeofSafety/ Seasonally-adjusted rail passenger miles - U.S. Department of Transportation, Bureau of Transportation Statistics (BTS) calculation from data collected by U.S. Department of Transportation, Federal Railroad Administration available at: safetydata.fra.dot.gov/OfficeofSafety/.

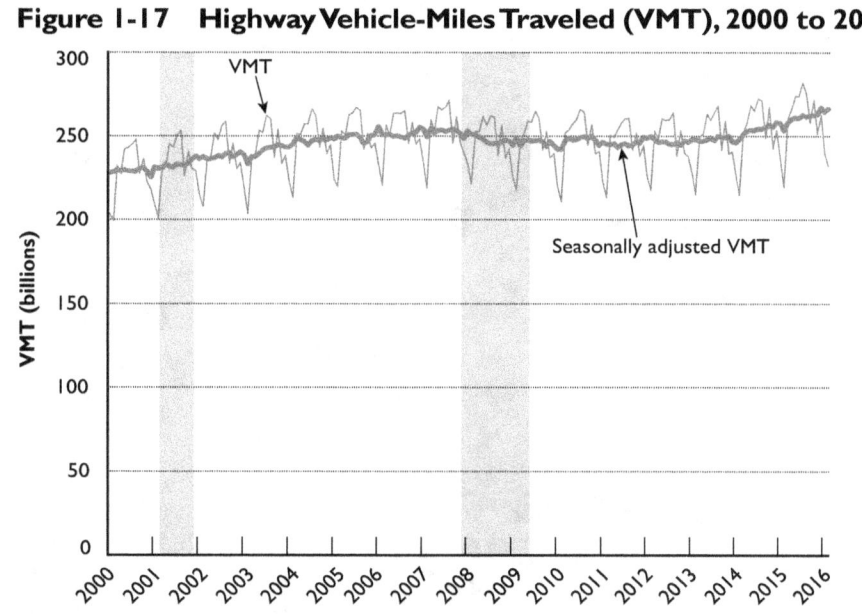

Figure 1-17   Highway Vehicle-Miles Traveled (VMT), 2000 to 2016

NOTE: Shaded areas indicate economic recessions.

SOURCES: U.S. Department of Transportation, Bureau of Transportation Statistics, seasonally adjusted transportation data, available at www.transtats.bts.gov/osea/seasonaladjustment/, as of May 2016.
Unadjusted VMT - U.S. Department of Transportation, Federal Highways Administration, Traffic Volumes and Trends www.fhwa.dot.gov/policyinformation/travel_monitoring/tvt.cfm.
Seasonally-adjusted VMT - U.S. Department of Transportation, Bureau of Transportation Statistics (BTS) calculation from U.S. Department of Transportation, Federal Highways Administration, Traffic Volumes and Trends www.fhwa.dot.gov/policyinformation/travel_monitoring/tvt.cfm.

2 TRANSPORTATION'S CONTRIBUTION TO THE ECONOMY

Introduction

Economic activity stimulates the use of transportation; transportation contributed 8.9 percent to the U.S. economy in 2014. Transportation is both an input to goods and services production and an output of consumed mobility and transportation vehicles purchased. This chapter uses data from the Bureau of Economic Analysis' National Income and Products Accounts to illuminate the economic contribution of transportation. Each section explains the meaning of, and discusses trends for, the following measurement concepts:

- Transportation-Related Final Demand

- For-Hire Transportation Services Produced in the Economy

- Transportation Satellite Accounts

All three measures illuminate the economic contribution of transportation. *Transportation-*

related final demand is a measure of the price paid for all transportation. *For-hire transportation services produced in the economy*, also called transportation value added, measures the value added to gross domestic product (GDP) by the transportation sector, using an input-output approach. Transportation Satellite Accounts supplement the value-added approach by incorporating transportation data provided by households and non-transportation firms.

Transportation-Related Final Demand

Gross domestic product (box 2-1) attributed to transportation-related final demand is a measure of the total value, or price paid, for all transportation regardless of the sector that produced the transportation goods or services. It includes the value of the inputs that transportation industries purchase, such as fuel, lubricants, equipment, parts, and

---

Box 2-1   National Income Account Terminology

The national income and product accounts use several related terms when discussing the size of the economy and sectors within the economy, such as transportation. These terms are used both in some of the figures in this chapter and other discussions of transportation economics.

- **What is Gross Domestic Product (GDP) and Gross Domestic Demand (GDD)?**

    ° *GDP* is the sum of the value of all goods and services produced in the U.S. economy.

    ° *GDD* is similar to GDP but excludes net exports, showing only domestic demand.

- **What are the differences among transportation value added, total transportation expenditures, transportation-related final demand, and the value of all shipments?**

    ° *Transportation Value Added* is a measure of the size

of the transportation sector based on the difference between the value of the transportation services sold and the goods and services used to produce transportation. The Bureau of Economic Analysis considers industry value added to be a measure of an industry's contribution to GDP.

    ° *Total Transportation Expenditure* measures what is spent on transportation without deducting the value of goods and services that are inputs. The main additional components are employee compensation and returns to capital.

    ° *Transportation-Related Final Demand* shows the impact of transportation as a factor in the demand for goods and services in the economy.

    ° *Value of Shipments* is the value of the goods transported by the freight transportation sector which is not the same as the value of the service of transporting them.

support services, as well as the value added by transportation industries themselves. Specifically, it includes the following key components:

- Gross Private Domestic Transportation Investment
- Government Transportation-Related Purchases
- Personal Consumption Expenditures
  - Motor vehicles and parts (purchases)
  - Motor vehicle fuels, lubricants and fluids (purchases)
  - Transportation services
- Net Exports of Transportation-Related Goods and Services

The transportation-related final demand data (box 2-2) summarize the final demand by households and government for transportation. Each input is counted in the sector that delivers final goods and services. This process provides information on all the pieces of aggregate demand directly related to transportation. If exports and imports of transportation-related goods and services were equal, i.e., if net exports were zero, then the total transportation-related GDP would be equal to the sum of domestic aggregate demand. However, recently imports have exceeded net exports so that net exports were negative every year. That is why graphical depictions of *transportation-related final demand* components show total transportation-related final demand including net exports as consistently below the sum of the domestic sources of demand.

Transportation-related final demand is not a perfect measure. For example, if investment in transportation infrastructure is below the level required to maintain the system's condition, then the measure will underestimate final demand. Transportation-related final demand does not include the full value of for-hire transport (mostly freight) as an intermediate good in the production of other goods. It does, however, include the capital expenditure used to produce

such services. Even with these shortcomings, transportation-related final demand can be used to compare the size of the transportation sector to that of other economic sectors such as healthcare and housing.

Box 2-2   Transportation-Related Final Demand

Transportation-related final demand is the most complete measure of transportation's role in the economy, specifically gross domestic product (GDP). Transportation-related final demand includes:

- For-hire transportation services
- Motor vehicle purchases
- Motor vehicle fuels, lubricants, and fluids
- Government transportation-related purchases
- Gross private domestic investment in transportation
- Net exports of transportation-related goods and services

Transportation-Related Final Demand by GDP Component

Figure 2-1 shows transportation-related final demand from 1999 to 2014 in chained 2009 dollars, and the pattern for each of the GDP components that make up final demand. Total transportation-related final demand trended upward from 1999–2007, but turned down dramatically during the 2008 and 2009 recession. The recessionary decline was most evident in private investment and personal consumption expenditure (purchases of motor vehicle fuels and parts, purchases of motor vehicle fuels, lubricants and fluids, and transportation services). Exports of transportation goods and services came close to balancing imports in 2009 (economic declines often reduce imports) but returned to their larger negative balance in subsequent years. Government transportation-related purchases peaked in 2003, and then declined steadily to $287.4 billion (in chained 2009 dollars) in 2008. They then rose in 2009 and 2010, as the government increased spending in response to the recession and to declines in private sector investment. Transportation-related final demand

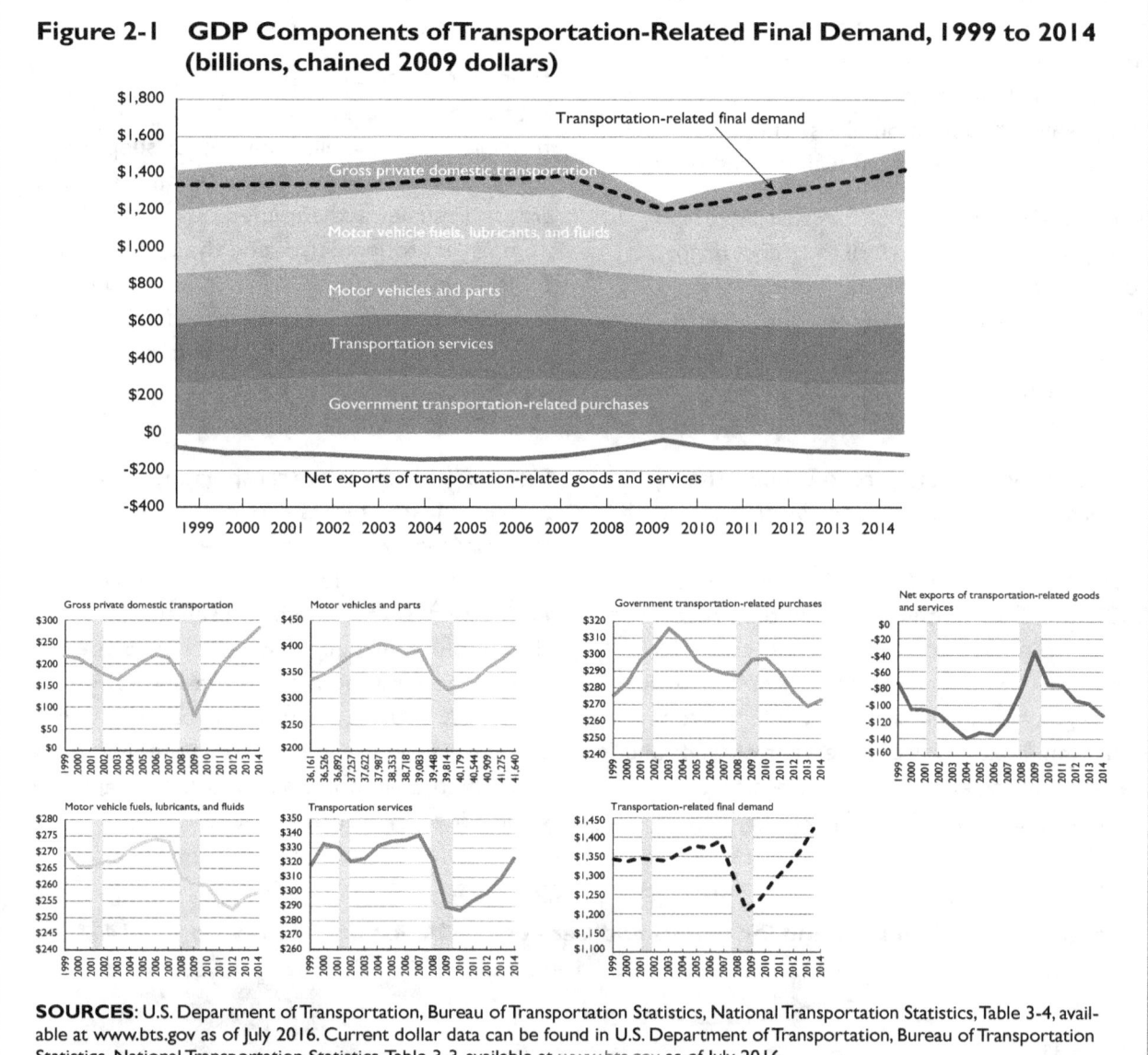

Figure 2-1   GDP Components of Transportation-Related Final Demand, 1999 to 2014 (billions, chained 2009 dollars)

SOURCES: U.S. Department of Transportation, Bureau of Transportation Statistics, National Transportation Statistics, Table 3-4, available at www.bts.gov as of July 2016. Current dollar data can be found in U.S. Department of Transportation, Bureau of Transportation Statistics, National Transportation Statistics, Table 3-3, available at www.bts.gov as of July 2016.

has increased since the recession to 2.3 percent above the 2007 pre-recession peak. The impact of the Great Recession on the transportation industry is demonstrated by the slow climb from the 2009 low to the 2014 level, only 6.0 percent above the 1999 level. For the transportation industry the Great Recession effectively removed over 10 years of growth in final demand. In 2014 the largest share of transportation-related final demand was motor vehicles and parts, as it was in

1999. Total transportation-related final demand in 2014 was $1.42 trillion (in chained 2009 dollars), compared to the BEA's value added in the for-hire transportation sector, which was $504.8 billion.

Gross Domestic Product (GDP) by Major Social Function

GDP by Major Social Function reflects broad economic activities, such as housing, transportation, and healthcare. The major social functions—housing, healthcare, food, transportation, and education—comprise 60 percent of GDP, while the 40 percent "other" category includes entertainment, personal care, and payments to pension plans. The size of each social function is based on final demand (box 2-2).

The wheel in figure 2-2 shows that in 2014 transportation was the fourth largest major social function after housing, healthcare, and food, representing 9.6 percent of total final demand. Housing is the largest single source of final demand in the U.S. economy, nearly twice the size of transportation.

The left-hand side of figure 2-2 shows the pattern of *GDP by major social function* over time. *Transportation-related final demand* decreased during the recession from 9.6 percent of GDP in 2007 to 8.2 percent in 2009, and then recovered slowly from 2009 to 2012, when it reached 9.7 percent of GDP. One can see the pre-recession housing bubble as housing peaked just before the recession, in 2005, at 22.4 percent of GDP, and declined during and after the recession to a low of 18.3 percent of GDP in 2012.

For-Hire Transportation Services Produced in the Economy

For-hire transportation services consists of the air, railroads, truck, passenger and ground transportation, pipeline, and other support services provided by transportation firms (e.g., transit agencies and common carrier trucking companies) to industries and the public on a fee basis. Calculating the GDP attributed to for-hire transportation uses a *value-added* approach that subtracts the cost of inputs (e.g., fuel and equipment costs) from total output (measured by sector revenue, e.g., airline fares).

Figure 2-3 shows how transportation ranks among industries in its economic output. Each industry sector has an estimated contribution to GDP based on its *value added* (box 2-3). All industry sectors together sum to GDP; thus, looking at their relative sizes shows where economic activity generating GDP occurred. Figure 2-3 shows the contribution of transportation in the context of other sectors and how the economy as a whole leverages the value added by transportation.

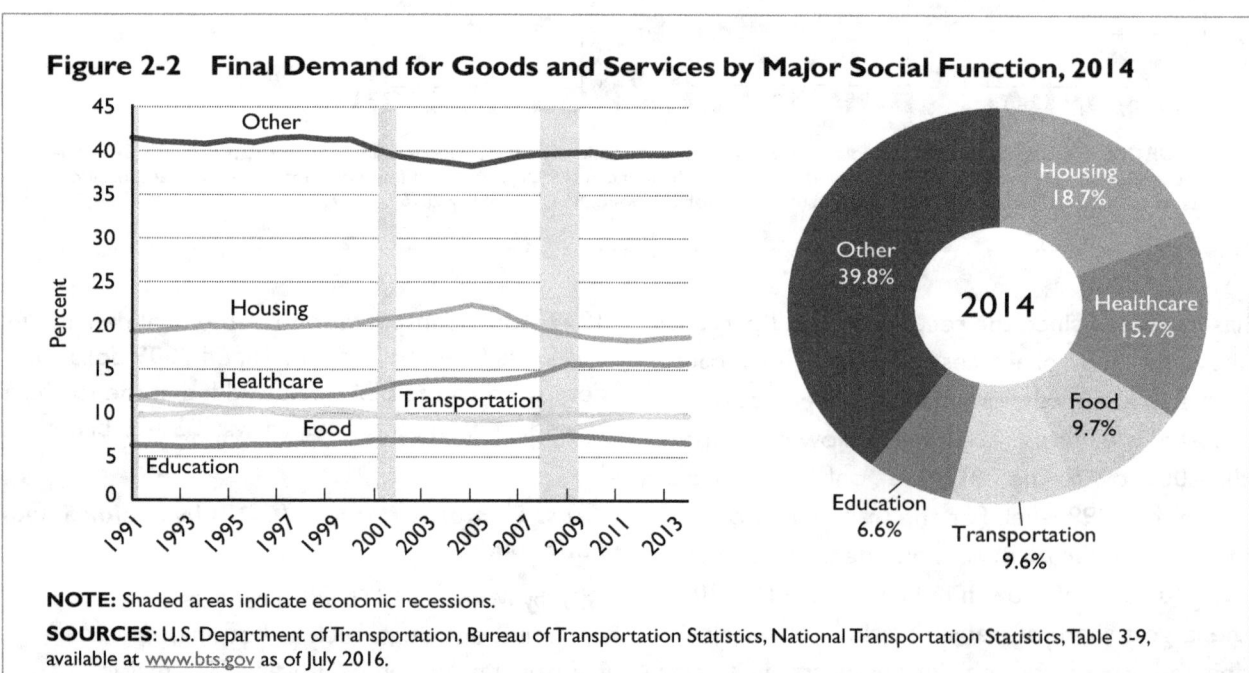

Figure 2-2   Final Demand for Goods and Services by Major Social Function, 2014

NOTE: Shaded areas indicate economic recessions.

SOURCES: U.S. Department of Transportation, Bureau of Transportation Statistics, National Transportation Statistics, Table 3-9, available at www.bts.gov as of July 2016.

Box 2-3   What is Value Added?

Transportation Value Added is a measure of the contribution of the transportation sector to gross domestic product (GDP) based on the difference between the value of the transportation services sold and the goods and services used to produce transportation. The Bureau of Economic Analysis (BEA) considers industry value added to be a measure of an industry's contribution to GDP..

The value of transportation sector outputs is estimated using data on the sales of transportation sector services to other parts of the economy. That shows what other parts of the economy are willing to pay for those services. In turn the transportation sector purchased inputs, such as fuel and equipment, are valued based on what the transportation

sector pays for them. The difference is the value added by the transportation sector, which is the transportation sector's contribution to GDP.

The contribution of the inputs to transportation includes the value added by the sector that produces them. For example, the contribution of the fuel purchased by for-hire carriers is included in the value added by the energy sector, which produced the fuel. It would be double counting the value added by fuel, if fuel purchased by for-hire transportation was not subtracted from the value added by transportation. Examples of other excluded inputs are equipment, spare parts, lubricants, and other materials.

This approach enables BEA to compute total GDP as the sum of the contributions of all sectors of the economy.

Figure 2-3 also highlights transportation and two transportation-reliant sectors (durable goods manufacturing and construction) sorted by industry sector contribution to GDP (on a value-added basis). Durable goods manufacturing is the largest of the three sectors (6.8 percent of GDP), followed by construction (3.8 percent) and transportation (2.7 percent). Transportation ranks 13th among the 17 industry sectors in terms of contribution to GDP.

This ranking likely, however, understates the

importance of transportation since all sectors rely on transportation, at least indirectly. To the extent that workers use the roadways to access customers and transit to commute, the ranking of the transportation industry is understated because there is no explicit payment for the full cost of those resources. There is also an understatement of the transportation industry ranking because in-house transportation (transportation undertaken by a business for internal use) is not included in the figure 2-3

Figure 2-3   Contribution to Gross Domestic Product (GDP) by Industry Sector, 2015

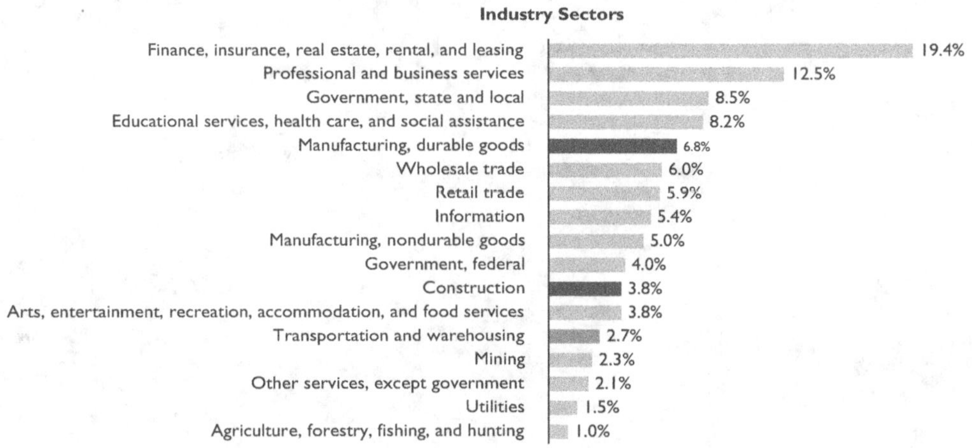

Industry Sectors

Industry Sector	Percent
Finance, insurance, real estate, rental, and leasing	19.4%
Professional and business services	12.5%
Government, state and local	8.5%
Educational services, health care, and social assistance	8.2%
Manufacturing, durable goods	6.8%
Wholesale trade	6.0%
Retail trade	5.9%
Information	5.4%
Manufacturing, nondurable goods	5.0%
Government, federal	4.0%
Construction	3.8%
Arts, entertainment, recreation, accommodation, and food services	3.8%
Transportation and warehousing	2.7%
Mining	2.3%
Other services, except government	2.1%
Utilities	1.5%
Agriculture, forestry, fishing, and hunting	1.0%

SOURCE: U.S. Department of Commerce, Bureau of Economic Analysis, GDP by Industry table "Real Value Added by Industry (A) (Q)", available at www.bea.gov/iTable/index_industry_gdpIndy.cfm as of July 2016.

industry sector ranking. This understatement is corrected by the *Transportation Satellite Accounts*, discussed later in this chapter, which adds transportation activity performed by non-transportation firms to the 2.7 percent contribution that is shown in figure 2-3.

The percentage that transportation and warehousing contributes to a state's GDP depends on the state's geography, population density, mix of industries, and location of transportation hubs (box 2-4). For example, Nebraska has a major national rail hub in Omaha, and has the second-highest percentage of GDP from transportation and warehousing of any state in the country (7.9% of GDP in 2015). States with larger total GDPs, such as California ($2.46 trillion) and New York

($1.44 trillion), also have large transportation and warehousing activities—$56.1 billion and $26.7 billion, respectively. Because other economic activities are so much larger in California and New York, however, transportation and warehousing is a relatively small share of their total GDP (figure 2-4).

Figure 2-5 breaks out the transportation contribution to GDP by mode and the patterns of change over time in each mode's percentage contribution to GDP. In 2014 the three modes with the largest contributions were trucking ($135.1 billion, 0.81 percent of GDP), other transportation and support activities ($112.3 billion, 0.56 percent) and air ($84.0 billion, 0.41 percent). The modes that grew as a percentage of GDP from 1997 to 2014 were water (from

Figure 2-4   State Gross Domestic Product from Transportation and Warehousing as a Percent of State Total Gross Domestic Product, 2015

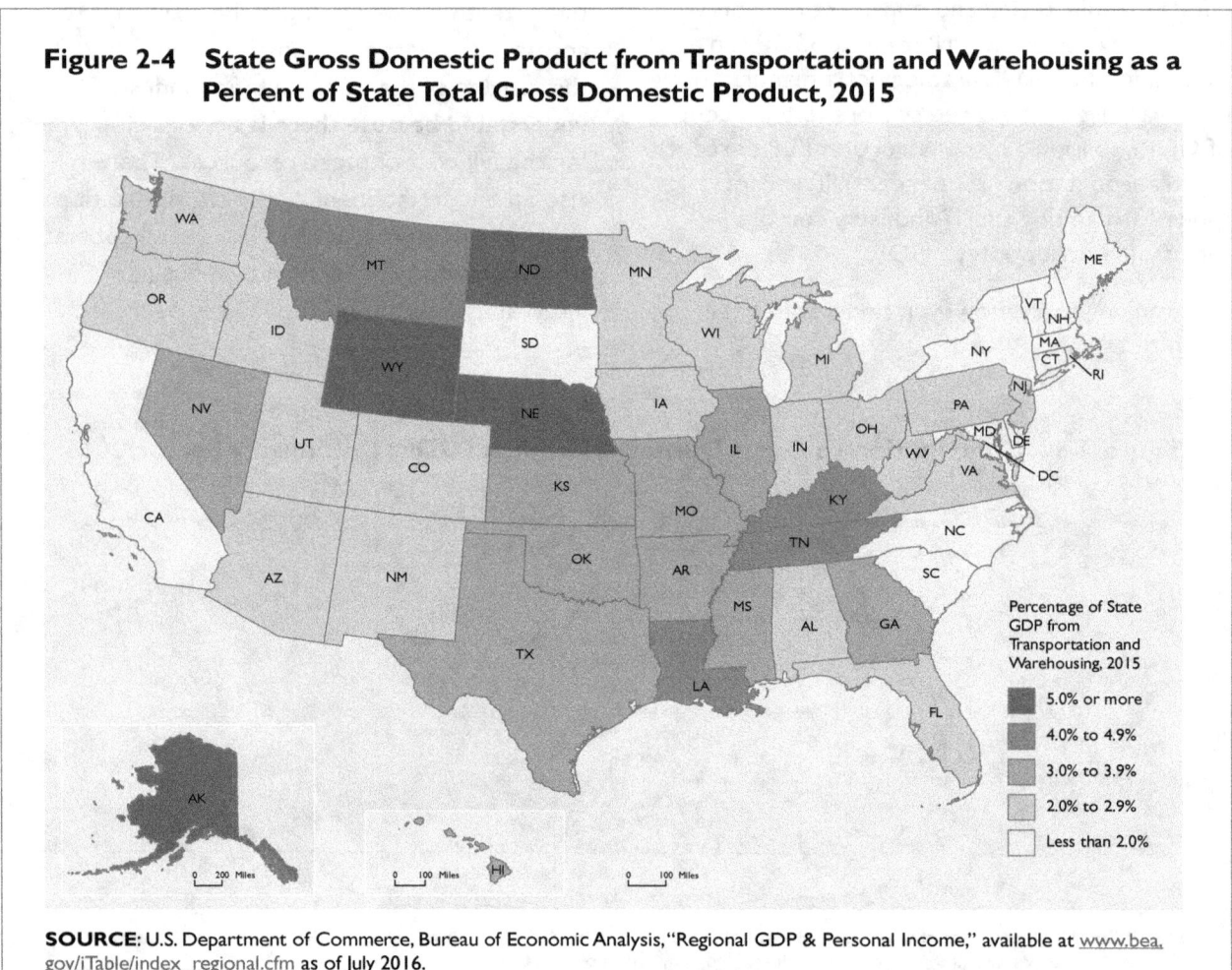

SOURCE: U.S. Department of Commerce, Bureau of Economic Analysis, "Regional GDP & Personal Income," available at www.bea. gov/iTable/index_regional.cfm as of July 2016.

Figure 2-5 For-Hire Transportation Industry's Contribution to GDP by Mode

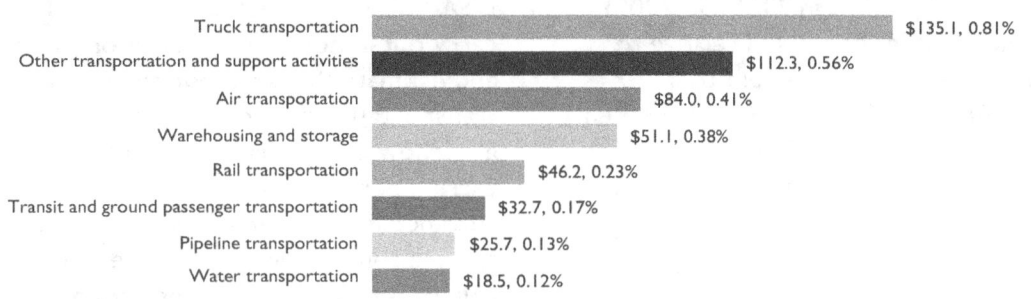

Contribution to national GDP, 2014 (billions of dollars, percent)

Truck transportation	$135.1, 0.81%
Other transportation and support activities	$112.3, 0.56%
Air transportation	$84.0, 0.41%
Warehousing and storage	$51.1, 0.38%
Rail transportation	$46.2, 0.23%
Transit and ground passenger transportation	$32.7, 0.17%
Pipeline transportation	$25.7, 0.13%
Water transportation	$18.5, 0.12%

Percent Contribution to GDP by Mode

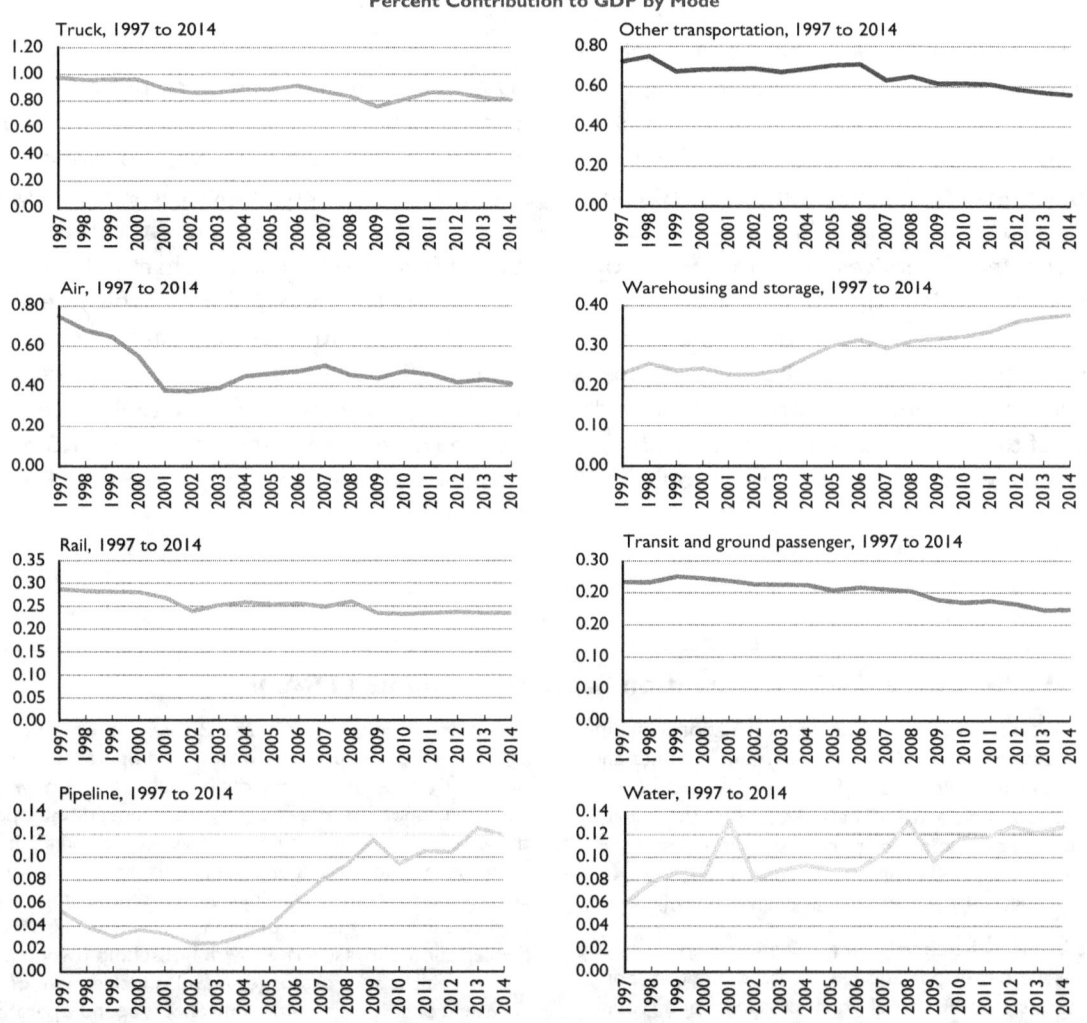

NOTES: Data are from the value added by industry table of the BEA Industry Economic Accounts. Data for Transportation and Warehousing is Line 40, and for individual modes are in Lines 41 through 48. Current dollar data can be found in NTS Table 3-1.

SOURCE: U.S. Department of Transportation, Bureau of Transportation Statistics, National Transportation Statistics, Table 3-2, available at www.bts.gov as of March 2014.

0.05 percent to 0.12 percent), warehousing and storage (from 0.23 percent to 0.38 percent), and pipelines (from 0.06 percent to 0.13 percent, with peaks of 0.13 percent in 2001 and 2008). However, most modes decreased relative to GDP—trucking (from 0.98 percent to 0.81 percent), air (from 0.75 percent to 0.41 percent), rail (from 0.29 percent to 0.23 percent), transit (from 0.22 percent to 0.17 percent), and other transportation (from 0.72 percent to 0.56 percent).

Transportation Satellite Accounts

The Bureau of Economic Analysis measures the value added by for-hire transportation using the Economic Census Survey. *For-hire transportation services* are produced by transportation firms (trucking companies, railroads, and airlines) and sold to transportation users. In addition to for-hire transportation services, non-transportation industries also produce transportation services for their own purposes. For instance, grocery stores may operate a truck fleet to move food from distribution centers to stores. BEA embeds the value of these services, known as *in-house transportation*, within the value of the goods

purchased by non-transportation industries to carry out in-house transportation operations. BTS developed the *Transportation Satellite Accounts (TSAs)* to extract the commodities used to carry out in-house transportation operations and estimate the contribution of in-house transportation to the economy. The TSAs also show the contribution of transportation carried out by households through the use of an automobile. The TSAs (box 2-5) thereby provide a more comprehensive measure of the size and role of transportation in the economy.

Transportation Satellite Account Results

The TSAs compute transportation's GDP contribution attributed to all transportation modes. In 2012, the latest year for which comprehensive data are available, transportation's total GDP contribution was estimated at $970 billion (figure 2-6). The pie chart in figure 2-6 represents total U.S. GDP, and the slice shows the portion contributed by transportation, based on the TSAs. The colors within the slice show the relative shares of for-hire (2.9 percent), in-house (1.2 percent), and household (1.8 percent) transportation's contribution to GDP. For-hire

---

Box 2-5   What are the Transportation Satellite Accounts (TSAs)?

Satellite industry accounts expand on the national income and product accounts and the input-output accounts, and supplement these accounts by focusing on a particular aspect of economic activity. The TSAs capture transportation activities carried out by non-transportation industries for their own purposes and transportation activities carried out by households through the use of an automobile.

The TSAs show the contribution of both for-hire, in-house, and household transportation services. *For-hire* transportation consists of the air, rail, truck, passenger and ground transportation, pipeline, and other support services provided by transportation firms such as railroads, transit agencies, common carrier trucking companies, and pipelines, to industries and the public on a fee-basis. *In-house* transportation consists of air, rail, water, and truck services produced

by businesses for their own use. Business in-house transportation includes privately owned and operated vehicles of all body types, used primarily on public rights of way, and the supportive services to store, maintain, and operate those vehicles. A baker's delivery truck is an example of business in-house transportation. Household transportation covers transportation provided by households for their own use through the use of a vehicle, measured by the depreciation cost associated with household ownership of motor vehicles. Air passenger travel is included in for-hire air transportation. The time households spend operating a private motor vehicle for personal use is not included, because it is not within the scope of the U.S. Input-Output (I-O) accounts, on which the TSAs are built. The I-O accounts, by design, do not include unpaid labor, volunteer work, and other non-market production.

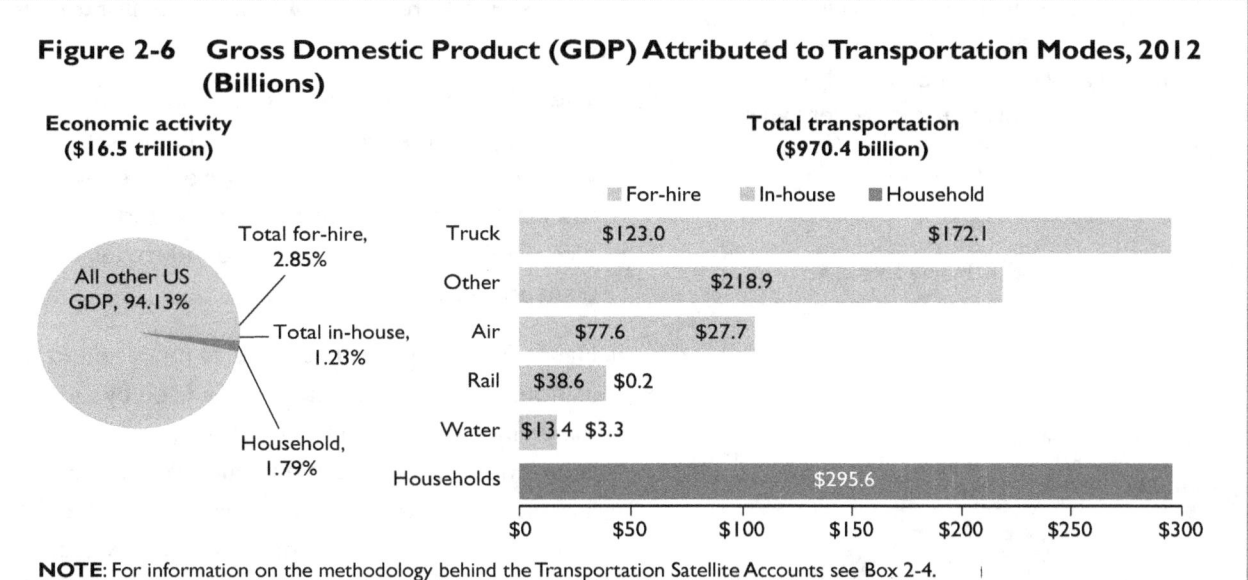

Figure 2-6 Gross Domestic Product (GDP) Attributed to Transportation Modes, 2012 (Billions)

NOTE: For information on the methodology behind the Transportation Satellite Accounts see Box 2-4.

SOURCES: U.S. Department of Commerce, Bureau of Economic Analysis, "Regional GDP & Personal Income," available at www.bea. gov/iTable/index_regional.cfm as of July 2016. U.S. Department of Transportation, Bureau of Transportation Statistics, Transportation Satellite Accounts, available at www.bts.gov.

transportation contributed $471.6 billion (2.9 percent) to the U.S. GDP of $16.5 trillion.[1] Transportation services (air, rail, truck, and water) provided by non-transportation industries for their own use (called in-house transportation) contributed an additional $203.2 billion (1.2 percent) to U.S. GDP.[2]

The bars in figure 2-6 show the contribution by mode, and how much of the contribution for each mode falls into the categories of for-hire, in-house, or household transportation. For example, transportation services provided by trucks contributed a total of $295.1 billion to GDP comprised of for-hire transportation services provided on a fee basis ($123 billion) and in-house transportation services provided by businesses for their own use ($172 billion). Trucking rises in relative size when in-house

trucking is added to for-hire trucking, reflecting the use of trucking fleets owned and operated by businesses—from local plumber's trucks to national fleets owned and operated by many retailers.[3] Air contributed a total of $105.2 billion, comprised of $78 billion of for-hire services, and $28 billion of in-house services; and water contributed $16.7 billion, comprised of $13.4 billion of for-hire services and $3.3 billion of in-house services.

Total household transportation (i.e., the depreciation cost associated with households owning motor vehicles) is larger than any of the other modes in terms of contribution to GDP, at $296 billion. The BEA approach in general excludes household production because there are challenges to computing the "price" or "value" of such things as a homecooked meal. For the TSA, BTS measures the contribution of household transportation to GDP as the depreciation of motor vehicles and does not include the value

---

[1] The GDP value in the TSAs is larger than the GDP value published in the National Accounts. because it includes the contribution of household transportation. Household transportation covers transportation provided by households for their own use through the use of a motor vehicle.

[2] For example, a grocery chain that operates its own truck fleet.

[3] Large retailers, such as Walmart and Target, are captured by BEA in the For-Hire Transportation Sector but smaller retailers are subsumed into the BTS in-house estimate.

of time spent driving. Including household transportation highlights the importance of household transportation provided by households for their own use through the ownership of a vehicle.

Figure 2-7 Use of For-Hire and In-House Transportation by Industry Sector, 2012 (Billions)

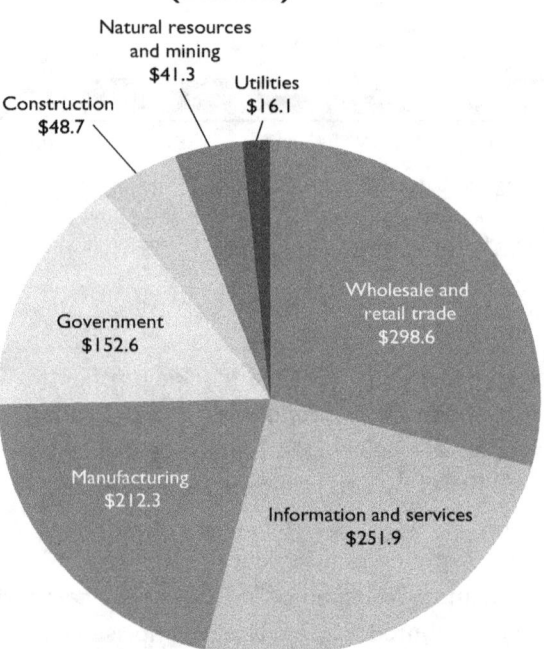

NOTE: The Transportation Satellite Accounts Use Table quantifies how transportation (both freight and passenger) is used by non-transportation sectors of the economy to create the goods and services that make up GDP. It includes in-house transportation activity (i.e., that which firms provide to move their own products) as well as for hire transportation. Data are shown by industry.

SOURCE: U.S. Department of Transportation, Bureau of Transportation Statistics, Transportation Satellite Accounts, available at www.bts.gov.

Use of For-Hire and In-House Transportation by Industry

The TSAs can also compute the extent of transportation services required to produce various goods and services. Figure 2-7 shows the relative importance of in-house and for-hire transportation as inputs to industries using transportation.

Figure 2-7 compares the value of for-hire and in-house transportation services used by seven major industries. When in-house transportation is included, wholesale and retail trade is the largest user of transportation services at $298.6 million, followed by information and services, and manufacturing. In the wholesale and retail trade industry, in-house transportation is 58 percent of the $299 billion total transportation services used (figure 2-8). Other sectors, such as manufacturing, are more reliant on for-hire transportation (in-house transportation is only 33 percent of the $212 billion total transportation services used by manufacturing). In-house transportation also represents a large portion of transportation services in natural resources/mining (49 percent of the $41 billion total transportation services used by natural resources/mining), in construction (61 percent of the $49 billion total transportation services), and in government (59 percent of the $153 billion total transportation services). BTS provides a full discussion of transportation's role in the seven major industry sectors in *Industry Snapshots: Transportation's Role in the U.S. Economy* available at bts.gov.

Figure 2-8   Use of For-hire and In-house Transportation by Industry Sector and Mode, 2012 (Billions)

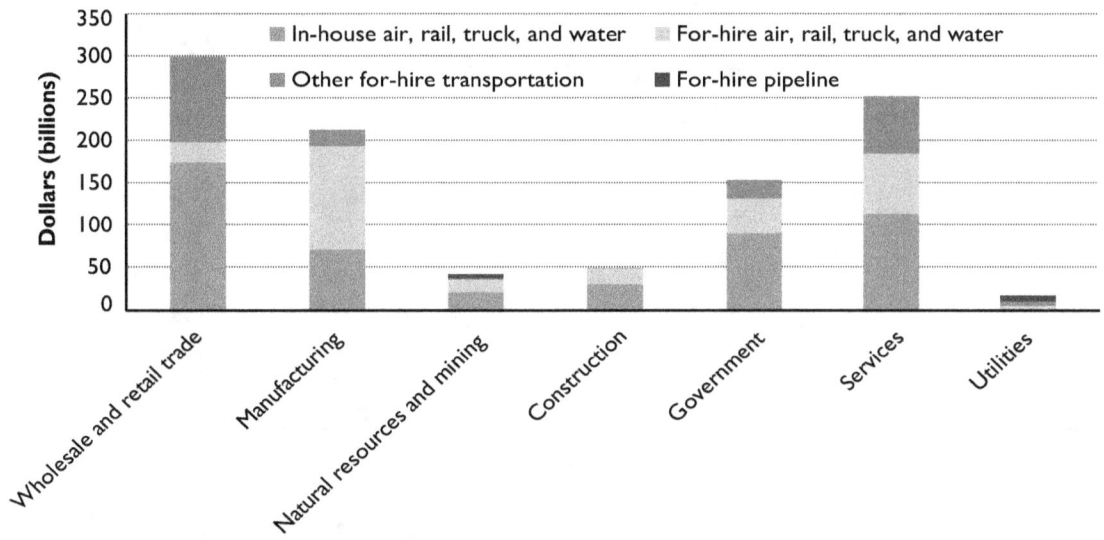

NOTES: The Transportation Satellite Accounts Use Table quantifies how transportation (both freight and passenger) is used by businesses in other sectors of the economy to create the goods and services that make up GDP. It includes in-house transportation activity (i.e., that which firms provide to move their own products) as well as for hire transportation. Data are shown by industry. Pipeline transportation is only shown separately for the Utility and Natural Resources industries. It is less than 5% of total transportation for other industries.

SOURCES: U.S. Department of Transportation, Bureau of Transportation Statistics, Transportation Satellite Accounts, available at www.bts.gov.

3   How Much Does Transportation Cost?

Transportation requires the use of resources—labor, equipment, fuel, and infrastructure. The cost of transportation is the use of these resources. Some of these resources are purchased directly by the users of transportation—for example, fuel purchased by households for automobile travel. Many resources are purchased by firms that provide transportation services—for example, labor purchased by a railroad or fuel bought by a trucking company. In addition, governments (federal, state and local) provide most of the transportation infrastructure, such as highways.

The prices transportation companies charge for transportation services become out-of-pocket costs to travelers and freight shippers, impacting their transportation choices. Because transportation is an input to the production of almost all goods and services, transportation price changes can influence the cost of other goods and services. Transportation prices themselves are impacted by the prices of inputs, such as labor costs, fuel costs, and the costs of transportation parts. This chapter discusses costs for three segments of the transportation market:

1. businesses that use transportation in production and delivery of non-transportation goods, such as retail and grocery;

2. producers of transportation services, such as railroads, airlines, or trucking companies; and

3. business and household travelers.

When disaggregate data are not available for business and household travelers, statistics that combine business and household travelers will be used. This chapter contains a special section on fuel because it is a key input to all transportation industries and households.

Finally, while businesses and households pay prices for transportation, the prices do not fully account for air pollution, traffic congestion, or other negative effects of transportation. These unaccounted effects represent costs to society, and are known as *negative externalities*. While negative externalities are an important part of economic analysis, this chapter covers only prices paid.

Costs to Use Transportation Services

This section presents data on transportation costs from two perspectives: (1) the *Producer Price Index* (PPI) (box 3-1) and (2) the *Consumer Price Index for all Urban Consumers* (CPI-U) (box 3-2). The PPI for a particular mode of transportation measures the average change in the selling prices received by producers of transportation services. Prices are from the point of view of the seller, and thus exclude items like sales and excise taxes. The CPI-U is a measure of the average change over time in the prices paid by urban consumers for a market basket of consumer goods and services.[1]

Producer Price Index

The *Producer Price Index* (PPI) shows the weighted average of wholesale or producer prices. Figure 3-1 shows PPIs in the transportation industry by mode from 2003 to 2015. Rail producer PPIs prices grew by 65 percent, more rapidly than any other transportation mode. Air and water PPIs also increased during this time period, with producer prices in trucking growing at a slightly slower rate than air and water. More research is needed to better understand the reasons why PPIs change differently by mode.

---

[1] The CPI-U excludes rural consumers to avoid statistical sampling issues.

Box 3-1   Producer Price Indices

The Producer Price Index (PPI) is the weighted average of wholesale or producer prices. These are the prices charged by producers of transportation services. The PPI for a particular mode of transportation measures the average change in the selling prices received by producers. For example the rail producer price index is based on a survey of railroad prices charged to shippers. The PPI for trucking services measures the average change over time in the selling price for trucking services. The PPI is different than the Consumer Price Index which shows changes in prices from the viewpoint of the consumer or purchaser of the transportation services.

The PPI is one of the most widely used measures of price

changes for the transportation sector and is published by the Bureau of Labor Statistics (BLS). BLS surveys a sample of individual business establishments. Because prices are from the point of view of the producer of transportation services, they exclude items like sales and excise taxes. Prices are weighted by the size of establishment's revenue to create indexes for narrowly defined services (such as local specialized freight trucking excluding used goods) and are then combined by BLS into aggregated indexes (such as all trucking) using value of shipments data from economic censuses of the Bureau of the Census. BLS publishes data for both broad and more narrowly defined services and costs.

SOURCE: U.S. Department of Transportation, Bureau of Transportation Statistics, 2016.

Box 3-2   Consumer Price Index for All Urban Consumers (CPI-U)

Consumer Price Index for all Urban Consumers (CPI-U) is a measure of the average change over time in the prices urban consumers paid for a market basket of consumer goods and services. Consumer Price Indexes (CPI) for particular goods and services, such as ones related to transportation, show changes in prices paid by consumers for transportation related goods and services. Comparing the CPI-U and

the CPI for transportation shows which transportation items are contributing to changes in the consumer cost of living, and comparing mode specific CPIs shows which modes of transportation are becoming more expensive relative to other modes of transportation.

SOURCE: U.S. Department of Transportation, Bureau of Transportation Statistics, 2016.

Figure 3-1   **Producer Price Indices for Providers of Selected Transportation and Warehousing Services, 2013–2015 (2003 = 100)**

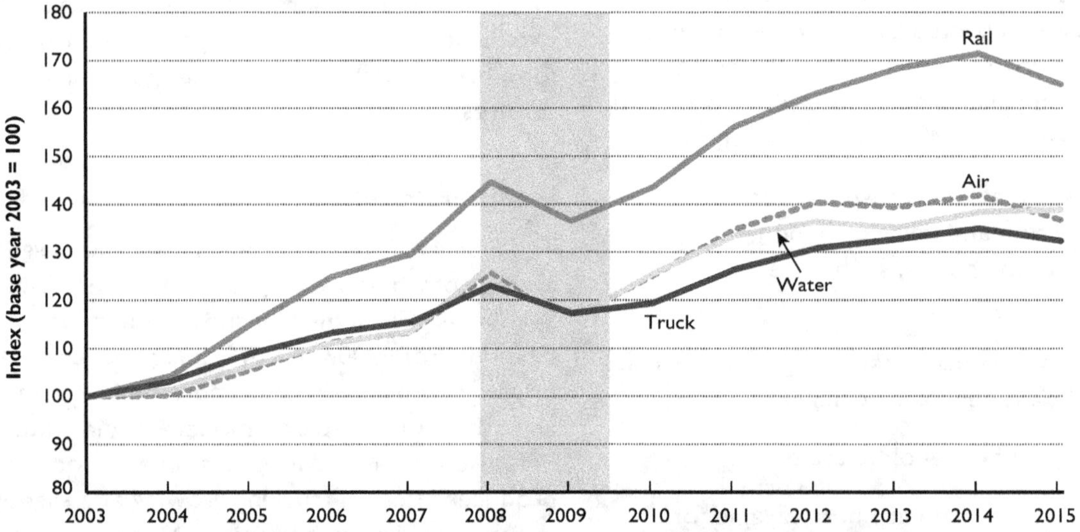

NOTES: Transportation Warehousing Services are defined on a North American Industry Classification System (NAICS) basis. Shaded bars indicate economic recessions.

SOURCES: U.S. Department of Transportation, Bureau of Transportation Statistics, *National Transportation Statistics*, Table 3-13, available at www.bts.gov as of August 2015.

The historic trends in the PPI show a peak across modes in 2008. The 2008 peak occurred at the end of a period of economic growth accompanied by increasing fuel prices. After a decline during the economic downturn in 2009, prices reached a new and higher level in 2011 and continued to increase through 2015. The rise in prices since 2009 has occurred during a period of economic growth.

Table 3-1 shows changes in producer prices for selected transportation industry subsectors. While transportation PPIs have often moved together, some subsectors show

Table 3-1 Detailed Producer Price Indices by Transportation Modes, 2003, 2007–2015

Mode	2003	2007	2008	2009	2010	2011	2012	2013	2014	2015
Air transportation (NAICS 481)[1]	162.1	183.7	203.8	188.5	202.9	218.3	227.6	226	230	221.7
Scheduled air transportation (NAICS 4811)[2]	198.5	224.5	248.9	229.1	247.7	267.9	280.1	278.3	283.8	272.5
Scheduled freight air transportation (NAICS 481112)	100	109	127.8	119.1	130.2	145.9	155.8	156.7	157	151.4
Nonscheduled air transportation (NAICS 4812)[3]	117.8	148.5	165.8	160.4	165.4	168.1	169.5	167.6	166.8	168.1
Rail transportation (NAICS 482)[3]	108.8	140.9	157.3	148.5	156.2	169.8	177.4	183.1	186.5	179.5
Line -haul railroads (NAICS 482111)[4]	121.4	157.2	175.5	165.6	174.3	189.4	197.9	204.2	208	200.2
Water transportation (NAICS 483)	100	113.5	127	116.1	125.5	133.4	136.4	135.1	138.4	138.9
Deep sea freight transportation (NAICS 483111)[5]	219.9	230	258.3	218.8	244.8	253.8	249.9	249.2	262.5	259.2
Coastal and great lakes freight transportation (NAICS 483113)	100	130.2	141.8	137.4	146.7	158.5	166.7	165.6	167.7	226.3
Inland water freight transportation (NAICS 483211)[6]	124.7	186.1	218.3	211.4	217.4	235.9	245.7	237.5	234.7	226.3
Truck transportation (NAICS 484)	100	115.4	123	117.3	119.4	126.4	130.8	132.7	134.9	132.3
General freight trucking (NAICS 4841)	100	116.5	123.6	117.5	119.3	126.8	132.4	134.7	137.5	134.9
General freight trucking, local (NAICS 48411)	100	119.6	130.2	126	127.2	130.5	132.8	135	135.2	135.1
General freight trucking, long distance (NAICS 48412)	100	115.9	122.2	115.5	117.5	126.1	132.4	134.7	138.1	134.9
Specialized freight trucking (NAICS 4842)	100	113.1	122.1	117.4	119.9	125.7	127.5	128.5	129.2	126.9
Used household and office goods moving (NAICS 48421)	100	108.8	112.2	112.8	114.7	122.9	124.4	124.9	126.7	126.1
Specialized freight (except used goods) trucking, local (NAICS 48422)	100	114.2	126.7	123.9	126.5	131.3	133.4	135.1	135.6	132.3
Specialized freight (except used goods) trucking, long distance (NAICS 48423)	100	114.8	123.6	113.2	115.8	121.4	122.9	123.4	123.9	121.6
Pipeline transportation (NAICS 486)	NA	NA	NA	NA	NA	NA	NA	NA	NA	NA
Pipeline transportation of crude oil (NAICS 4861)	100	125.4	137.1	141	183.4	184.7	195.5	211.1	222.6	233
Other pipeline transportation (NAICS 4869)	100	115	121.6	128.7	133.8	137.3	144.7	150.7	160.4	168
Support activities for transportation (NAICS 488)	100	108.5	111.7	108.6	110.7	114	115.7	117.5	118.7	118.7
Support activities for water transportation (NAICS 4883)	100	112.7	117.3	116.8	120.2	123.9	128	130.4	131.7	132
Postal service (NAICS 491)[2]	155	171.9	178.9	185	187.7	190.6	195.7	202.4	213.2	216.5
Couriers and messengers (NAICS 492)	100	131.5	142	141.5	153.4	168.8	179.7	189.4	198.3	203.2

NOTES: "NAICS" stands for "North American Industry Classification System." Federal statistical agencies use NAICS as the standard for classifying businesses when they collect, analyze, and publish economic data. Index base years are as follows: [1]Base year = 1992. [2]Base year = 1989. [3]Base year = 1996. [4]Base year = 1984. [5]Base year = 1988 [6]Base year = 1990. All others are base year 2003. NA = not available.

SOURCE: U.S. Department of Transportation, Bureau of Transportation Statistics, National Transportation Statistics, Table 3-13, available at www.bts.gov as of July 2016.

exceptions. Transportation prices declined for all transportation modes in 2009 during the recession, except the "household and office moving" subsector of the trucking industry, which saw a modest increase in prices (0.5 percent). Overall the PPI for water transportation increased from 2013 to 2015 (135.1 to 138.9), but during the same time the PPI for inland water freight transportation declined (237.5 to 226.3).

Consumer Price Index for Urban Consumers

The *Consumer Price Index for Urban Consumers* (CPI-U) is a measure of the average change over time in the prices paid by urban consumers for a market basket of consumer goods and services.

Economists often use the CPI-U (box 3-2) as an indicator of general price trends.

Consumer Price Indexes for particular goods and services, such as ones related to transportation, show changes in prices for those goods and services. Table 3-2 shows price changes in private and public transportation from 2014 to 2015. On average, transportation cost less in 2015 than in 2014 (table 3-2).

The *CPI-U* (box 3-2) for both private and public transportation declined from 2014 to 2015 (table 3-2). Costs for private transportation declined by 8.2 percent resulting primarily from a 27.1 percent decrease in gasoline cost as well as decreases in the cost of other fuels and

Table 3-2 Consumer Price Indexes for All Urban Consumers, Transportation Related Goods and Services

Goods and Services	2014 average	2015 average	Change from 2014 to 2015
Overall transportation	215.9	199.1	-7.8%
Private transportation	211.0	193.7	-8.2%
New and used motor vehicles [1]	100.8	100.8	-0.0%
New vehicles	146.3	147.1	0.6%
Used cars and trucks [1][2]	149.1	147.1	-1.3%
Motor fuel	292.4	213.1	-27.1%
Gasoline (all types)	290.9	212.0	-27.1%
Other motor fuels [1]	276.7	197.5	-28.6%
Motor vehicle parts and equ.	144.8	144.2	-0.4%
Tires	128.0	126.5	-1.2%
Motor vehicle maint. and repair	266.0	270.7	1.8%
Motor vehicle insur.	437.2	460.6	5.4%
Motor vehicle fees [1]	176.5	178.9	1.4%
Parking fees and tolls [1][2]	210.4	215.9	2.6%
Public transportation	276.4	268.7	-2.8%
Airline Fare	307.7	292.2	-5.0%
Other intercity	152.9	152.9	-0.0%
Intercity train fare [2][3]	111.1	110.0	-1.0%
Ship fare [1][2]	61.2	61.8	0.9%
Intracity transportation	297.4	303.9	2.2%
Intracity mass transit [2][4]	117.5	120.2	2.3%

NOTES: Based for indexes are as follows: [1]Indexes on a December 1997=100 base. [2]Special index based on a substantially smaller sample. [3]Indexes on a December 2007=100 base. [4]Indexes on a December 2009=100 base. All others, average of 1982 to 1984=100.

SOURCE: U.S. Department of Labor, Bureau of Labor Statistics, *CPI Detailed Report*, Table 1A and 3A, Data for January 2016 available at www.bls.gov/cpi/cpid1601.pdf as of July 2016.

tires. These decreases were partially offset by increases in the cost of insurance, parking fees and tolls, and vehicle maintenance and repairs. The 2.8 percent decline in public transportation costs reflected lower intercity costs for rail travel (-1.0 percent) and air (-5.0 percent). On the contrary, intracity transportation costs increased 2.2 percent, while intracity mass transit costs increased 2.3 percent from 2014 to 2015.

Fuel Prices

Fuel prices are a cost to transportation industries and a direct cost to consumers. The cost of petroleum products is a large share of the total value of the output of for-hire transportation services, ranging as high as 24 percent for aviation and 21 percent for trucking (figure 3-2). Gasoline and motor oil also account for 27.2 of household spending on transportation, as discussed in

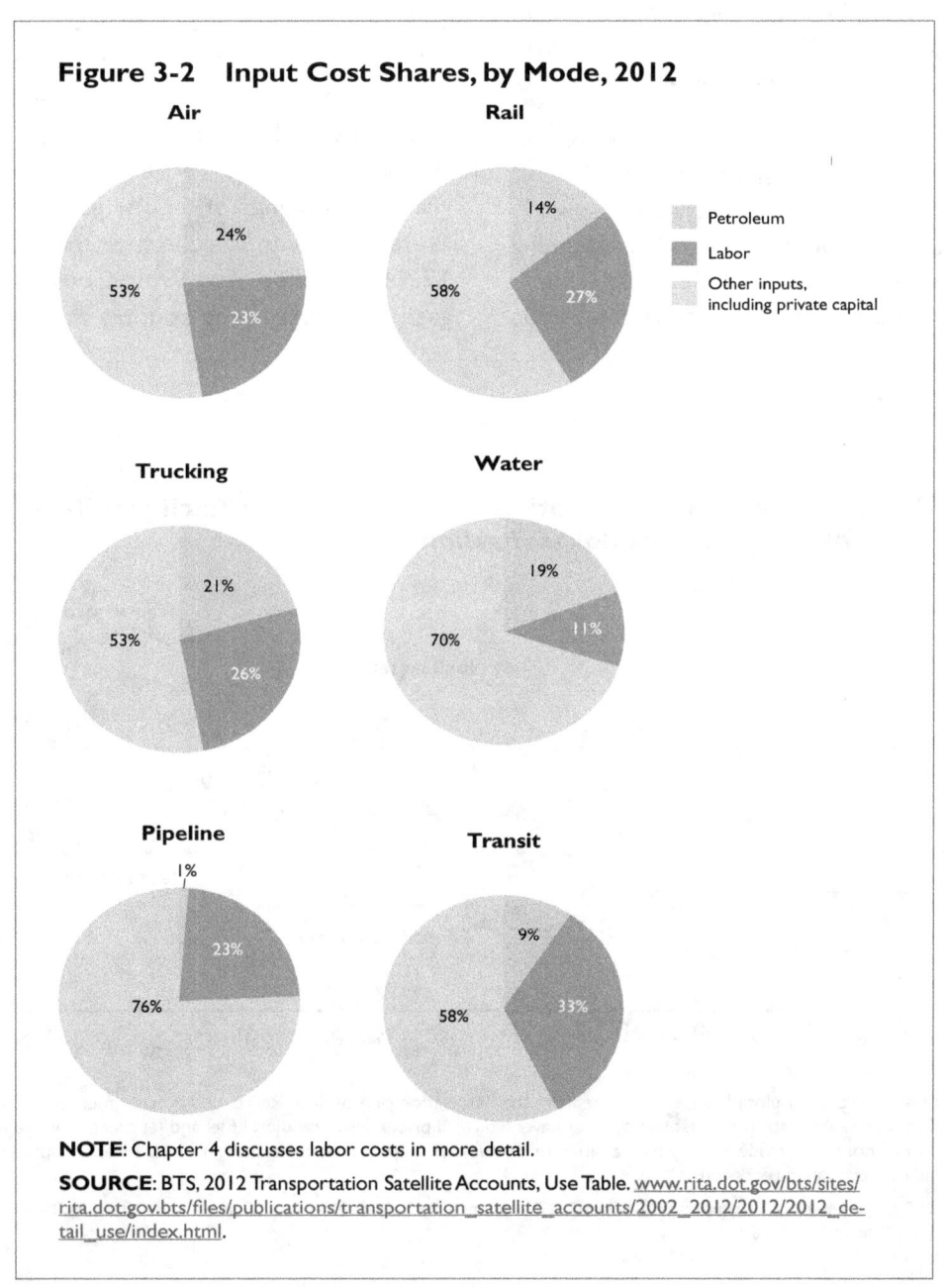

Figure 3-2   Input Cost Shares, by Mode, 2012

Air — 24%, 53%, 23%
Rail — 14%, 58%, 27%

Legend: Petroleum; Labor; Other inputs, including private capital

Trucking — 21%, 53%, 26%
Water — 19%, 70%, 11%

Pipeline — 1%, 23%, 76%
Transit — 9%, 58%, 33%

NOTE: Chapter 4 discusses labor costs in more detail.

SOURCE: BTS, 2012 Transportation Satellite Accounts, Use Table. www.rita.dot.gov/bts/sites/rita.dot.gov.bts/files/publications/transportation_satellite_accounts/2002_2012/2012/2012_de-tail_use/index.html.

Chapter 6. Fuel cost is very visible to households, as news reports focus on changes in fuel prices and gas stations (by law) must post prices, making fuel prices salient to consumers in ways other prices are not.

Sales Price of Transportation Fuel

Prices for regular gasoline, No. 2 diesel (used by automobiles and trucks), jet fuel kerosene, and railroad diesel typically move together with slight variations (figure 3-3). This reflects the underlying price of crude oil from which they all are refined.

Following a decade of relatively stable fuel prices in the 1990s, fuel prices began to increase. Gasoline, No. 2 diesel fuel, and kerosene spiked to over $3.00 per gallon in 2008. While declining sharply during the recession of 2008-2009, fuel prices began to rise again, rising above the 2008

price just after 2011. Since peaking in 2012, prices declined in 2013 through 2015. In 2015 prices declined sharply below 2009 levels for diesel fuel and kerosene, and just above 2009 levels for gasoline.

Average Motor Gasoline Prices by Region

Gasoline prices vary substantially across the United States. Prices can vary because of state and local taxes, refinery locations, fuel supplies, retail competition, and fuel regulations. Figure 3-4 illustrates average regional gasoline prices in 2015 using data from the Energy Information Administration (EIA). The averages include all grades and blends of regular gasoline. In 2015 the average gasoline price in the United States was $2.52 per gallon. The West Coast had the highest gasoline prices in the country at $3.04 per

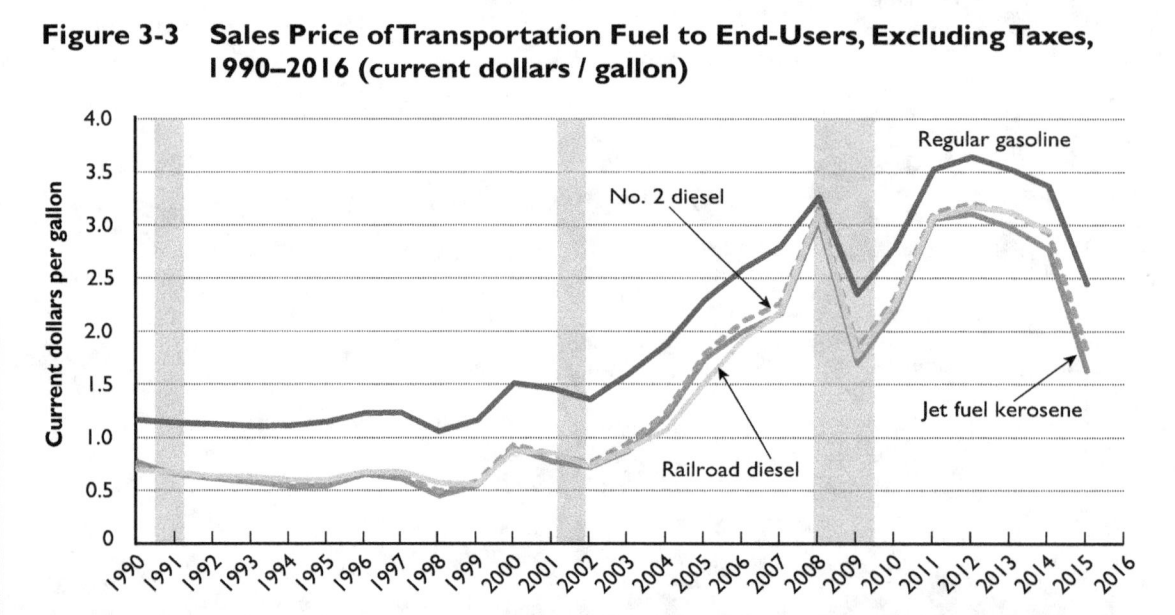

Figure 3-3   Sales Price of Transportation Fuel to End-Users, Excluding Taxes, 1990–2016 (current dollars / gallon)

NOTES: Data on the cost of railroad diesel fuel come from the Association of American Railroads. All other fuel cost data come from the Energy Information Administration. Gasoline costs are average retail prices. Highway diesel fuel and jet fuel prices are based on sales to end-users (those sales made directly to the ultimate consumer, including bulk customers in agriculture, industry, and utility). Shaded bars indicate economic recessions.

SOURCES: U.S. Department of Transportation, Bureau of Transportation Statistics, *National Transportation Statistics*, Table 3-11, available at www.bts.gov as of July 2016.

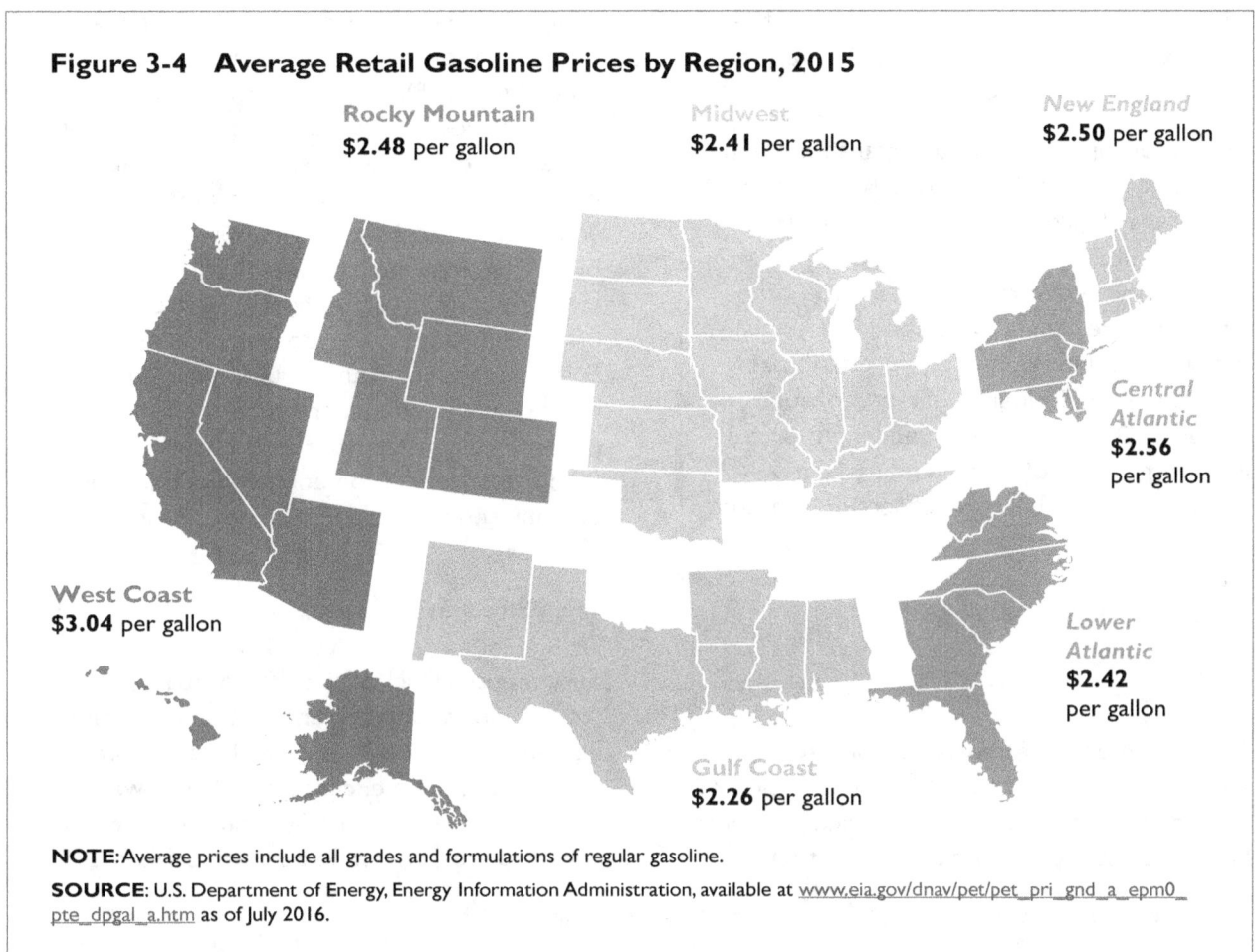

Figure 3-4 Average Retail Gasoline Prices by Region, 2015

Rocky Mountain
$2.48 per gallon

Midwest
$2.41 per gallon

New England
$2.50 per gallon

Central Atlantic
$2.56 per gallon

West Coast
$3.04 per gallon

Lower Atlantic
$2.42 per gallon

Gulf Coast
$2.26 per gallon

NOTE: Average prices include all grades and formulations of regular gasoline.

SOURCE: U.S. Department of Energy, Energy Information Administration, available at www.eia.gov/dnav/pet/pet_pri_gnd_a_epm0_pte_dpgal_a.htm as of July 2016.

gallon—$0.50 more than the Central Atlantic, which had the second-highest prices at $2.56 per gallon. Prices were highest in California, at $3.13 per gallon, because California requires a unique blend of gasoline to meet environmental regulations. Meanwhile, the Gulf Coast had the lowest gasoline prices at $2.26 per gallon, or $0.15 lower than the Midwest, which had the second-lowest prices at $2.41 per gallon.

Costs to Deliver Transportation Services

There are two types of transportation services: freight transportation services provided to producers of goods and services (e.g., trucking and air freight); and passenger transportation services provided to both producers and household consumers. The price of freight transportation services is a cost to producers of many goods and services, and thus impacts the prices of those goods and services. The cost of passenger transportation services directly impacts consumers as well as the prices of goods and services because producers also use passenger transportation services to conduct business.

The cost to produce transportation goods and services is measured using a variety of economic sources, such as producer price indexes for inputs, average wages, and fuel prices. From the perspective of the input producers (e.g., oil and gas companies, vehicle manufacturers), input prices represent a source of revenue for their products; but from the point of view of the transportation service providers, input prices are costs. Those costs impact the profitability of transportation firms and the prices that transportation firms charge users for transportation services.

The major inputs to produce transportation services are labor, fuel, materials, and supplies as well as the depreciation of items like airplanes, trucks, railroad locomotives and freight cars, trucking terminals, railroad track, and other infrastructure. The depreciation represents the reduction in an asset's value attributable to wear and tear, accidental damage, obsolescence, and aging. The depreciation and input prices impact the price of freight and passenger transportation. The next subsection presents a measure of equipment costs to the producers of transportation services. Measures of labor costs are presented in chapter 4.

Equipment Cost

Different modes of transportation use different equipment. This equipment is primarily privately owned by the transportation service providers. Specific price indexes for transportation

equipment show how the producers' price of transportation-related equipment changes over time (figure 3-5). The Producer Price Index (PPI) includes indexes for equipment used by transportation industries, such as aircraft, railroad cars, and heavy trucks, as well as equipment used by consumers, such as vehicles owned by households. The PPI shows the trends in transportation equipment manufacturing prices and reflect their potential impact on the cost of delivering transportation services— the higher the equipment cost, the higher the cost of delivery transportation services. The PPI for transportation equipment should not be confused with the PPIs for transportation services.

The PPIs for transportation equipment, which include indexes for automobile and light duty motor vehicles, aircraft, railroad rolling stock, ships and boats, and all transportation equipment, showed an upward trend from 2003 to 2015. An exception to this upward trend is automobile and light duty motor vehicle prices, which decreased between 2003

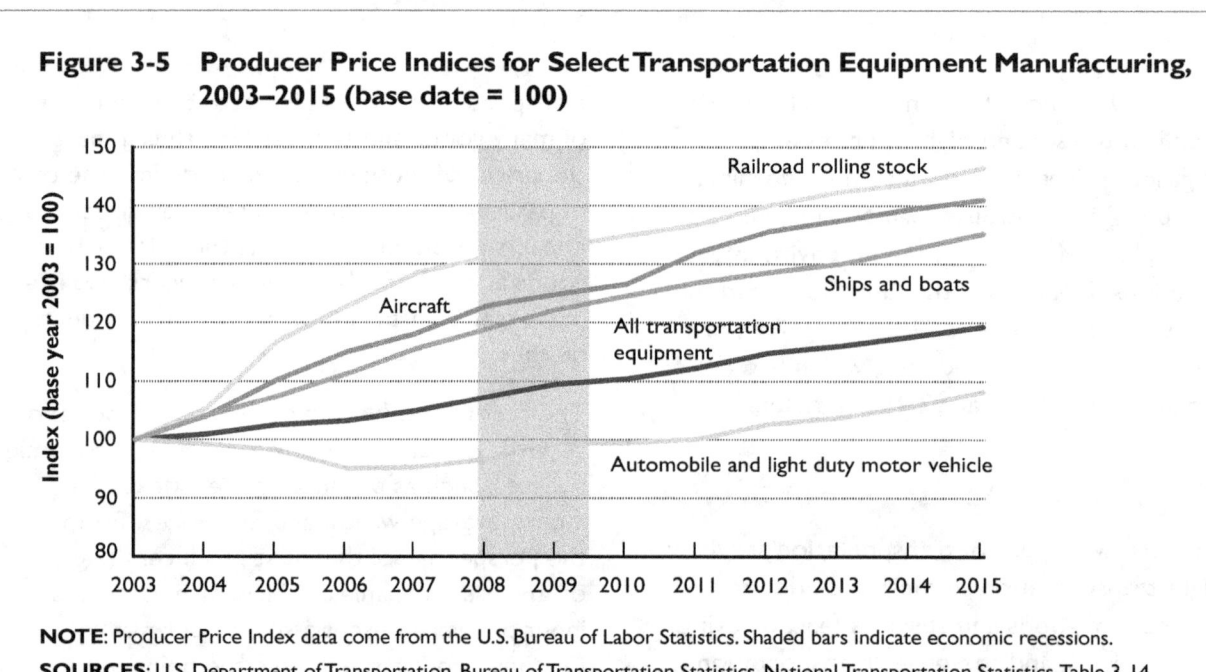

Figure 3-5   Producer Price Indices for Select Transportation Equipment Manufacturing, 2003–2015 (base date = 100)

NOTE: Producer Price Index data come from the U.S. Bureau of Labor Statistics. Shaded bars indicate economic recessions.

SOURCES: U.S. Department of Transportation, Bureau of Transportation Statistics, National Transportation Statistics, Table 3-14, available at www.bts.gov as of July 2016.

and 2008, leveled off from 2009 to 2011, and finally increased from 2012 through 2015. The PPIs for railroad, aircraft, and ship and boat manufacturing showed a growth greater than that for all transportation equipment combined. This increase in equipment prices potentially impacted the profitability and purchase decisions of transportation sectors, the transportation costs for transportation users, and prices along the economic supply chain in other sectors that use transportation services, such as wholesale, retail, and warehousing and storage industries.

Costs of For-Hire Travel

Households pay for travel in two ways. First, they pay fares to use for-hire passenger transportation services, as discussed below. Second, they pay to own and operate passenger vehicles for their own use, as discussed in chapter 6 on household transportation expenditures. For-hire passenger transportation services provide *intercity* and *intracity* travel.

For-hire intercity passenger transportation consists of three modes—aviation, rail,[2] and scheduled bus service[3] other than that provided by transit agencies (e.g., Greyhound, Bolt Bus and Megabus) (box 3-3). For-hire intracity travel includes local transit and commuter rail. Local and commuter passengers typically travel much shorter distances than intercity passengers. For example, the average trip length for intercity rail was 39.5 miles according to the 2009 NHTS, while the average trip length for transit was 7.2 miles.

Aviation Fares

Adjusted for inflation, passenger airfares decreased by 28 percent from 1993 to 2009, but increased over 4.3 percent since 2009 (figure

---

[2] Intercity rail service provided by Amtrak – commuter rail services are included with other intracity modes in Intracity Passenger Fares.

[3] Up to date fare data on intercity bus is not currently available, and so is not included in this document.

Box 3-3 Average Fares

Providers of for-hire passenger transportation services such as airlines, railroads, and transit agencies charge a variety of fares for different services. The average fare for a mode is defined as the sum of all fare revenue received by the service providers in that mode, divided by the number of one-way trips.

Data on revenue and trips for air come from the U.S. Department of Transportation, Bureau of Transportation Statistics, Office of Airline Information. Revenue is divided by trips. Baggage fees are not included in passenger revenue and free flights such as frequent flyer rewards are not included in trips.

Data on revenue and trips for rail come from Amtrak's Annual Report. The annual report gives ticket revenue per passenger mile which is multiplied by average trip length of passengers.

Data on commuter rail and transit come from the Federal Transit Administration's National Transit Database. For transit the revenue is divided by unlinked trips. Trips on transit often involve transfers between two buses, or a bus and rail transit. Many transit systems are only able to capture the number of boardings, and cannot link the segments into a complete one way trip, so unlinked trips (i.e., the number of times a passenger boards a transit vehicle) is used instead. If data on complete one way trips were available, it would show somewhat higher average fares for transit.

SOURCE: U.S. Department of Transportation, Bureau of Transportation Statistics, 2016.

3-6). Average airfares were $412 in 1993 and declined to $334 in 1999 before recovering to $396 in 2000. In the following decade they dropped to a low of $297 in 2009 before slowly rebounding to $327 in 2014, and decreasing to $315 in 2015. All changes are shown in real chained dollars, which account for inflation and substitutions within market baskets. Fares do not include baggage or reservation fees, which airlines began to charge in 2008.

Domestic air travel includes relatively short trips of under 700 miles and trips as long as 3500 miles. Figure 3-7 shows that throughout the period from 2009 to 2015 air fares have been related to distance traveled and air fares by different distances have had similar patterns over time. Change in air fares between 2009 and

Figure 3-6 Domestic Air Fares (scheduled service), 1993 to 2015

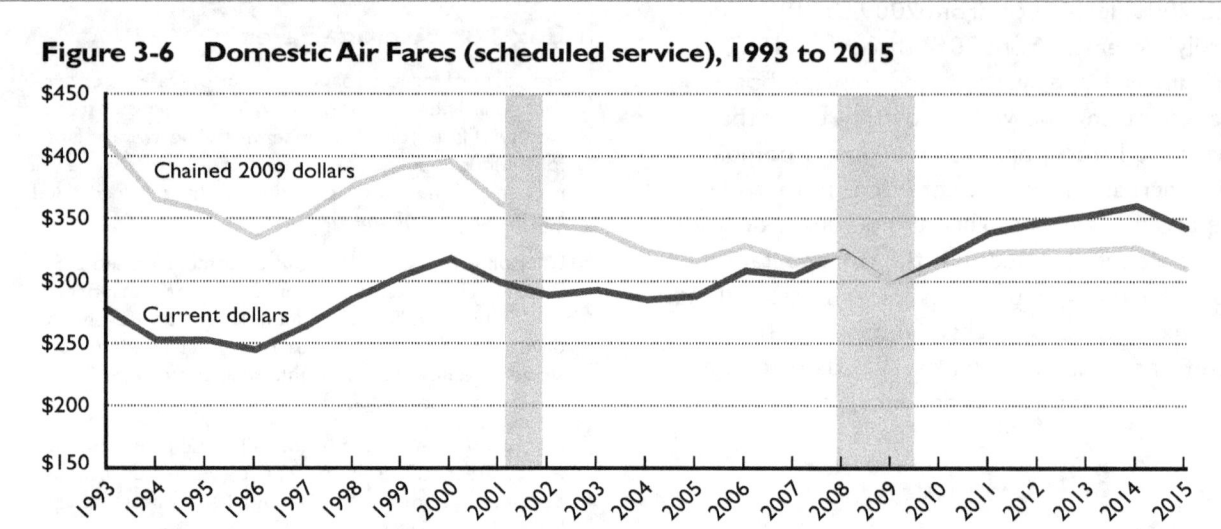

NOTES: Domestic Air Carrier Fare: Data are from the U.S. Department of Transportation, Bureau of Transportation Statistics, Office of Airline Information, TranStats Database, T1: U.S. Air Carrier Traffic and Capacity Summary by Service Class and Air Carrier Financial Reports, Schedule P-11 and Schedule P-12. National Transportation Statistics Table 3-19 takes total revenue from these sources and divides by total trips to arrive at average fare. Fares do not include baggage fees or reservation change fees, which airlines began charging in 2008. Shaded bars indicate economic recessions.

SOURCES: U.S. Department of Transportation, Bureau of Transportation Statistics, *National Transportation Statistics*, Table 3-18, available at www.bts.gov as of July 2016.

Figure 3-7 Domestic Average Air Fares by Distance Traveled (current dollars), 2009 to 2015

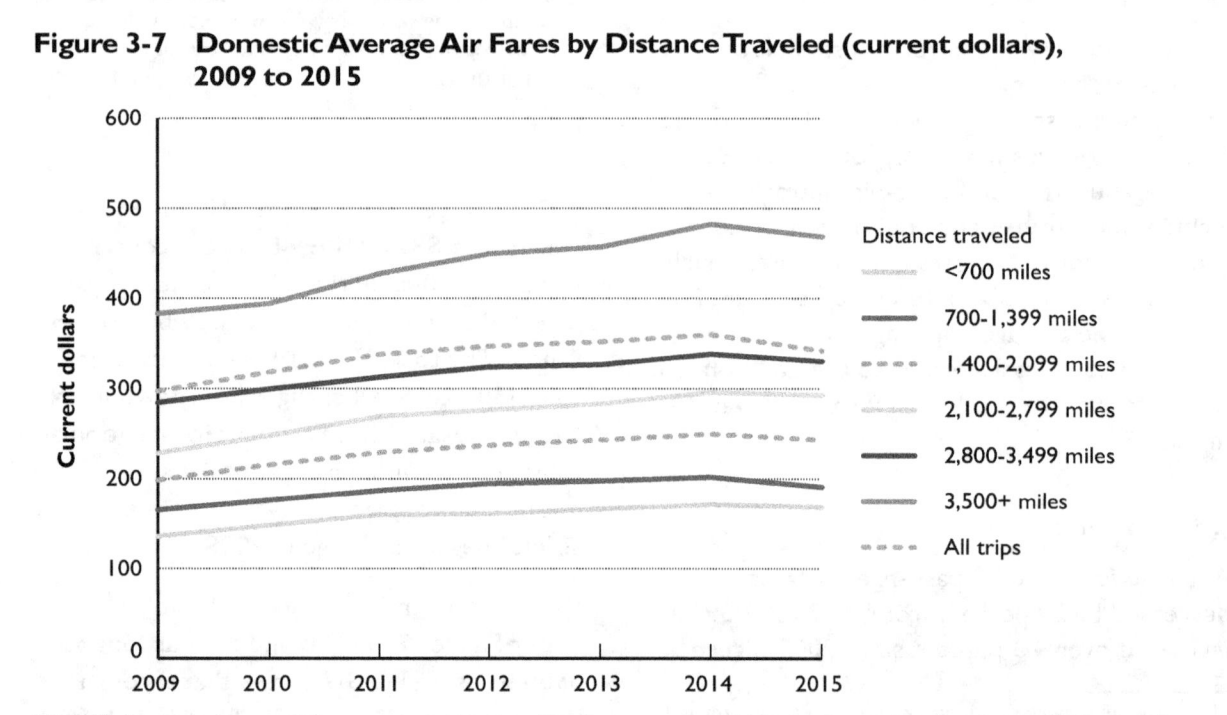

NOTES: Domestic Average Air fares are determined by taking the revenue and dividing by the number of passengers. Airfare includes base fare plus taxes paid by the passenger at the time of ticket purchase. The data represent a 10% sampling of tickets obtained upon the passenger's first traveled segment. The fare does not include any additional items such as baggage fees, airline lounge access, and seat upgrades.

SOURCES: U.S. Department of Transportation, Bureau of Transportation Statistics, Office of Airline Information, 2016.

2015 ranged from an increase of 15.6 percent for trips between 700 and 1400 miles, to an increase of 28.2 percent for trips between 2100 and 2800 miles. Fares peaked in 2014 for all distance categories.

Intercity Railroad Fares

Amtrak intercity railroad fares represent a complex interaction of demand, operating costs, government subsidies, and regulation. Amtrak fares (in chained 2009 dollars) fluctuated within a narrow band from 1990 to 2013 (figure 3-8). The fares represent ticket revenue per passenger mile multiplied by average trip length of passengers except for years prior to 1997 where fares are calculated from total transportation revenues. Amtrak fares fell from about $59 per passenger in 1991 to $52 in 1995 and fluctuated between $52 and $61 from 1995 through 2003. Passenger fares began to rise again in 2004, hitting a peak

of about $62 in 2007. Fares declined during the recession but returned to $62 in 2013.

Commuter Railroad Fares

Commuter rail is railway passenger service that operates between a central city and adjacent suburbs. Intercity rail service such as Amtrak is excluded, except for that portion of service operated by or under contract with a public transit agency for predominantly commuter services. Predominantly commuter service means that for any given trip segment (i.e., distance between any two stations), more than 50 percent of the average daily ridership makes a return trip on the same day. Commuter rail does not include heavy rail rapid transit or light rail/streetcar transit service. Figure 3-9 shows that commuter rail fares peaked at just over $5.00 (in chained 2009 dollars) in 2013, following a decade of increases after a low-point in 2002.

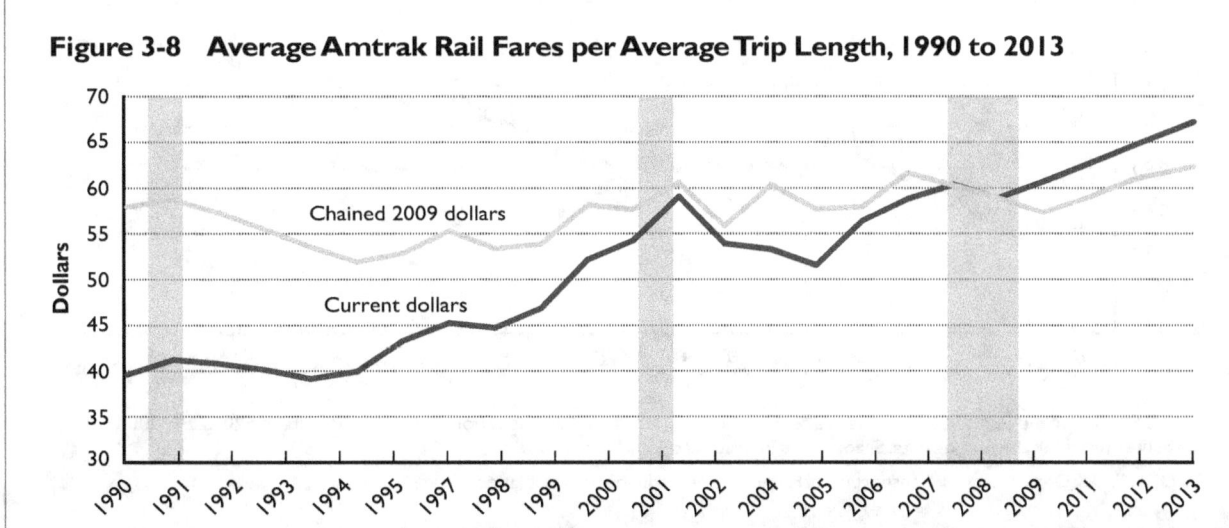

Figure 3-8   Average Amtrak Rail Fares per Average Trip Length, 1990 to 2013

NOTES: InterCity Rail/Amtrak Fare: 1997-2013: National Passenger Rail Corporation (Amtrak), Amtrak Annual Report (Washington, DC: Annual Issues) (ticket revenue per passenger mile multiplied by average trip length of passengers) For years prior to 1997 calculated as total transportation revenues / Amtrak system passenger trips, from National Passenger Rail Corporation (Amtrak), Amtrak Annual Report, Statistical Appendix (Washington, DC: Annual Issues). Shaded bars indicate economic recessions.

SOURCE: Intercity Rail/Amtrak: U.S. Department of Transportation, Bureau of Transportation Statistics, *National Transportation Statistics*, Table 3-19, available at www.bts.gov as of July 2016.

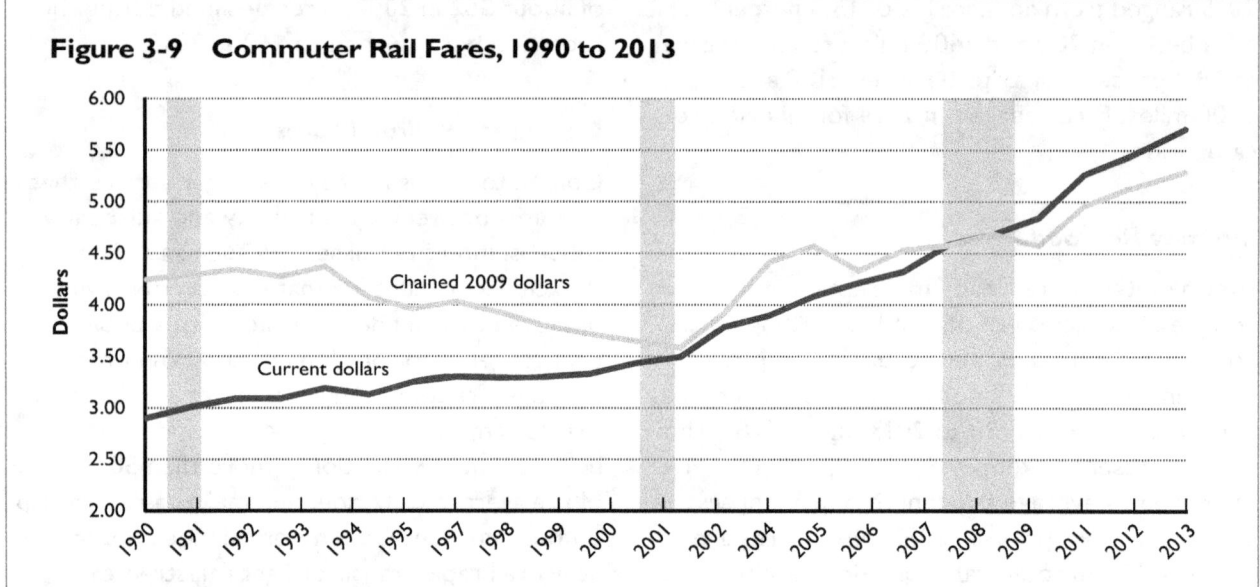

Figure 3-9   Commuter Rail Fares, 1990 to 2013

NOTE: Shaded bars indicate economic recessions.

SOURCE: U.S. Department of Transportation, Bureau of Transportation Statistics, *National Transportation Statistics*, Table 3-18, available at www.bts.gov as of July 2016.

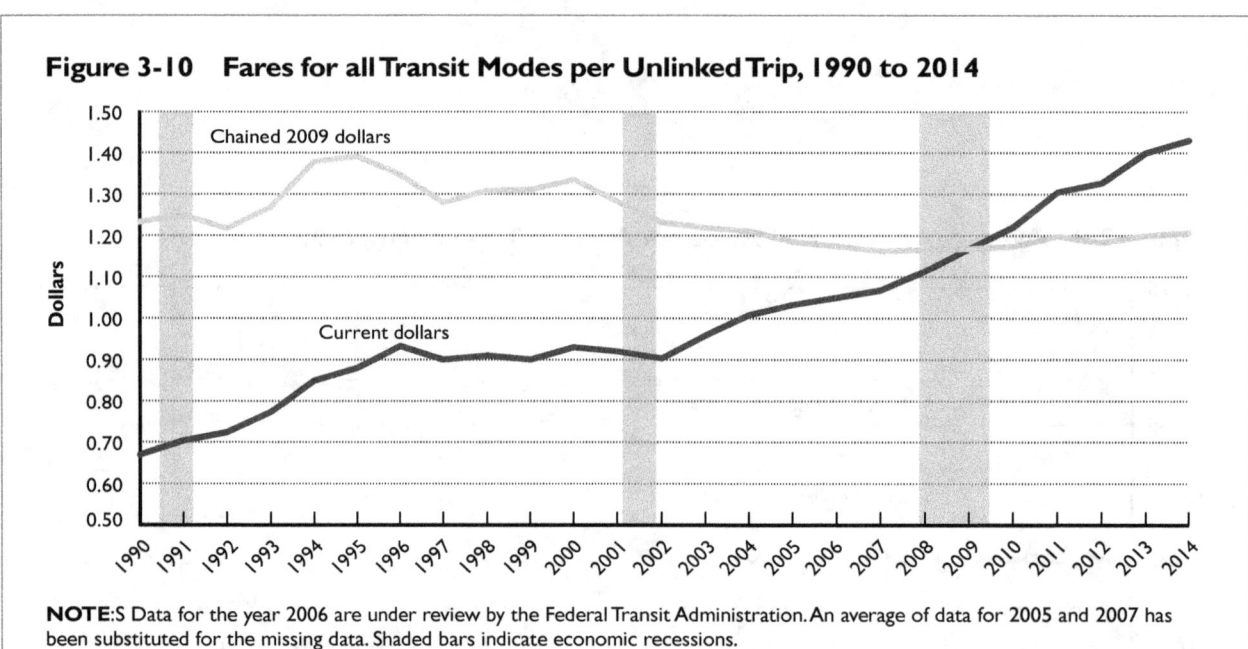

Figure 3-10   Fares for all Transit Modes per Unlinked Trip, 1990 to 2014

NOTE:S Data for the year 2006 are under review by the Federal Transit Administration. An average of data for 2005 and 2007 has been substituted for the missing data. Shaded bars indicate economic recessions.

SOURCE: U.S. Department of Transportation, Federal Transit Administration, National Transit Database.

Transit Fares

Transit modes include heavy rail (subway or metro), light rail, bus, and trolley car. Local transit fares in chained 2009 dollars have fluctuated between $1.16 and $1.39 per unlinked trip over the last two decades, declining only 2 percent in that period (figure 3-10).[4]

_____

[4] Transit cost is based on the average fare per unlinked trip. For example, if a passenger takes a bus at a fare of $1, to a subway station and then takes the subway at a fare of $2, this would be two unlinked trips with an average fare of $1.50.

Transit fare is per unlinked trips. Unlinked trips means that a trip involving a bus to train transfer, for example, would be counted twice. Many transit agencies are unable to reflect the existence of transfers in counting trips.

4 TRANSPORTATION EMPLOYMENT

The transportation and warehousing sector and related industries employ over 13.1 million people in a variety of roles, from driving buses to manufacturing cars to building and maintaining ports and railroads (box 4-1). This chapter explores transportation employment by industry, occupation, mode, and state, and highlights the significant role that transportation employment plays in the Nation's job profile.

> **Box 4-1   Sectors, Subsectors, and Industries**
>
> Terms like "sector" and "industry" are often used interchangeably. For precision, this chapter uses the terms in the same manner as the North American Industry Classification System (NAICS). In NAICS, sectors contain subsectors, subsectors contain industry groups, and industry groups contain industries, as shown in the following example:
>
> **Sector**: Transportation and warehousing (NAICS 48-49)
>
> **Subsector**: Truck transportation (NAICS 484)
>
> **Industry group**: General freight trucking (NAICS 4841)
>
> **Industry**: General freight trucking, long-distance (NAICS 48412)
>
> **Industry detail**: General freight trucking, long-distance, less than truckload (NAICS 484122)
>
> **SOURCE**: Bureau of Transportation Statistics, 2016.

Transportation-Related Employment in the United States

Figure 4-1 shows the number and percent of workers in transportation-related industries from 1990 to 2014. "Transportation-related industries" includes all industries in the transportation and warehousing sector, as well as related industries like motor vehicle parts manufacturing. In 1990, 12.3 million workers were employed in these industries. Employment rose to a high of 13.9

million workers in 2000, but declined to 13.2 million by 2003 following the 2001 recession. Employment declined further to 12.1 million in 2010 due to the 2007 to 2009 recession. While employment has risen to 13.1 million as of 2014, it has yet to rise above the prerecession level of 13.5 million in 2007. At the same time, however, the percentage of American workers in transportation-related employment declined from 11.3 percent in 1990 to 9.4 percent in 2014.

Transportation Employment by Industry and Occupation

Employment in the For-Hire Transportation and Warehousing Sector

The for-hire transportation and warehousing sector directly employs nearly 4.6 million workers in the United States—over 3 percent of the nation's total labor force. Employment in this sector involves a number of occupations and covers a diverse set of skills. Figure 4-2 compares employment by the for-hire transportation and warehousing sector to employment in related areas such as retail trade (a major user of both for-hire and in-house transportation), the Postal Service (another important user of transportation), and government (which is involved in many aspects of transportation) (box 4-2).

Figure 4-3 shows for-hire transportation and warehousing employment from 1990 to 2014 by subsector (box 4-3). Each subsector exhibits different patterns of employment because they have a different mix of job skills and occupations as well as economic environments. For some subsectors, employment has grown from 1990 to 2014. For example, truck transportation employment grew by 26 percent between 1990 and 2014, from 1.1 million to 1.4 million

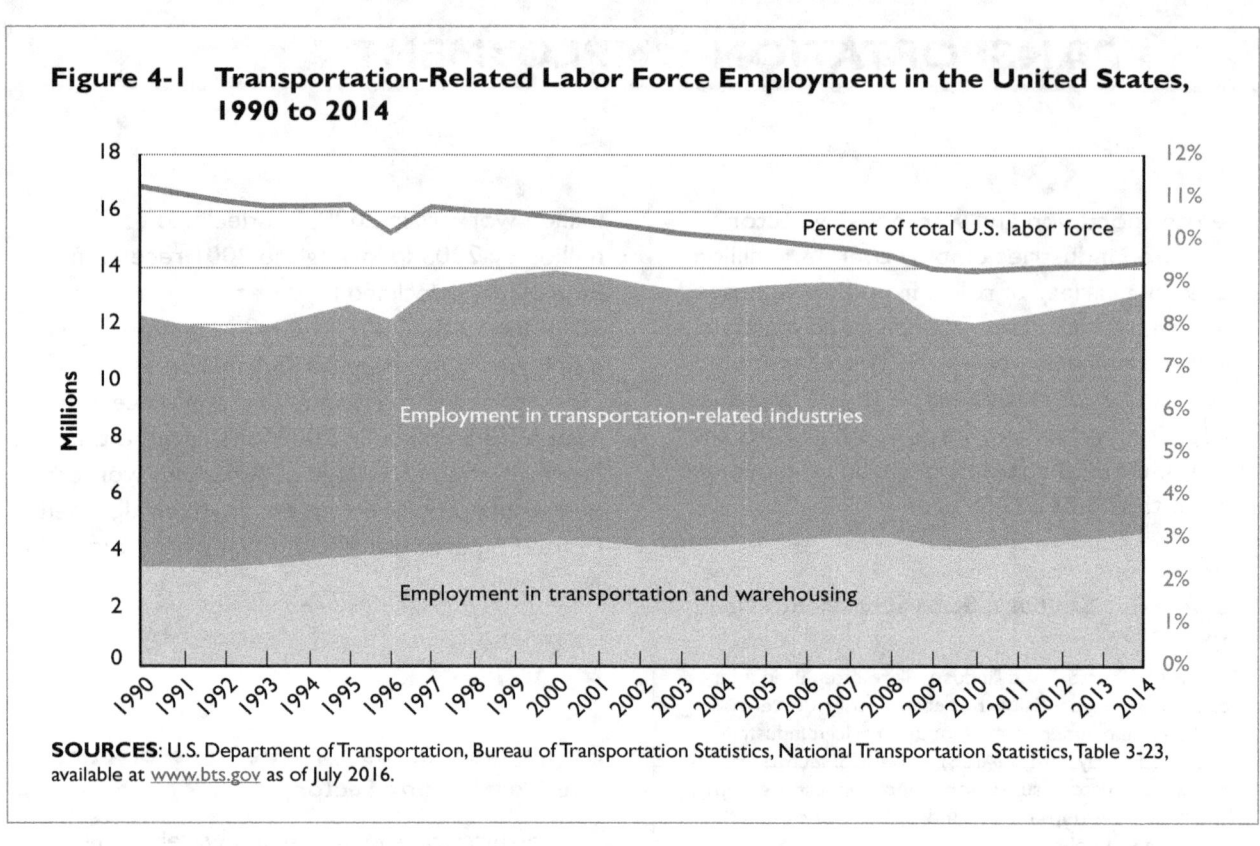

Figure 4-1   Transportation-Related Labor Force Employment in the United States, 1990 to 2014

Percent of total U.S. labor force

Employment in transportation-related industries

Employment in transportation and warehousing

SOURCES: U.S. Department of Transportation, Bureau of Transportation Statistics, National Transportation Statistics, Table 3-23, available at www.bts.gov as of July 2016.

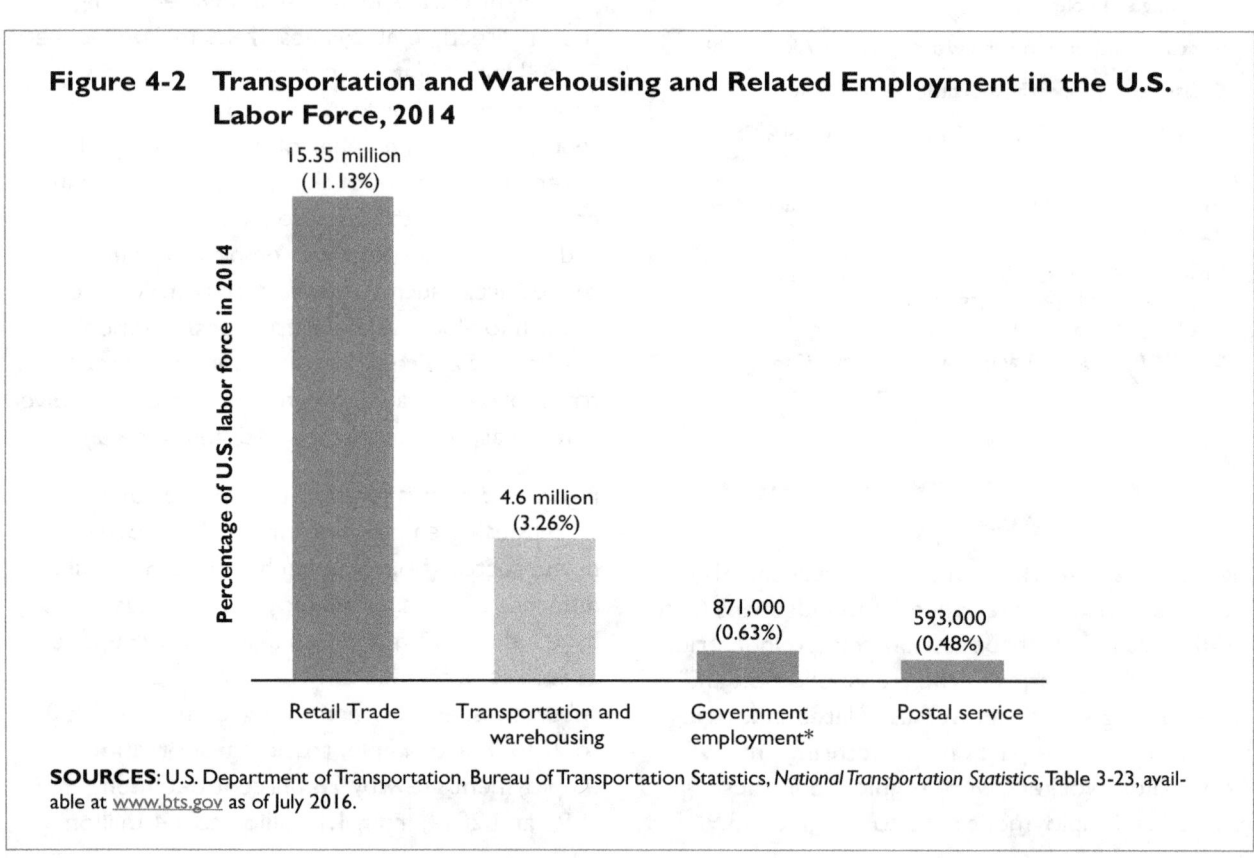

Figure 4-2   Transportation and Warehousing and Related Employment in the U.S. Labor Force, 2014

15.35 million
(11.13%)

4.6 million
(3.26%)

871,000
(0.63%)

593,000
(0.48%)

Retail Trade   Transportation and warehousing   Government employment*   Postal service

SOURCES: U.S. Department of Transportation, Bureau of Transportation Statistics, *National Transportation Statistics*, Table 3-23, available at www.bts.gov as of July 2016.

Box 4-2   For-Hire and In-House Transportation

For-hire transportation consists of transportation services provided on a fee basis to industries and the public. These services are provided by businesses such as railroads, transit agencies, common-carrier trucking providers, airlines, and pipeline companies.

In-house transportation consists of the services provided by non-transportation industries for their own use. It in-cludes privately owned and operated vehicles used primarily on public rights of way, as well as the supportive services to store, maintain, and operate those vehicles.

SOURCE: Bureau of Transportation Statistics, 2016.

Figure 4-3   Employment in For-Hire Transportation by Subsector (thousands), 1990 to 2014

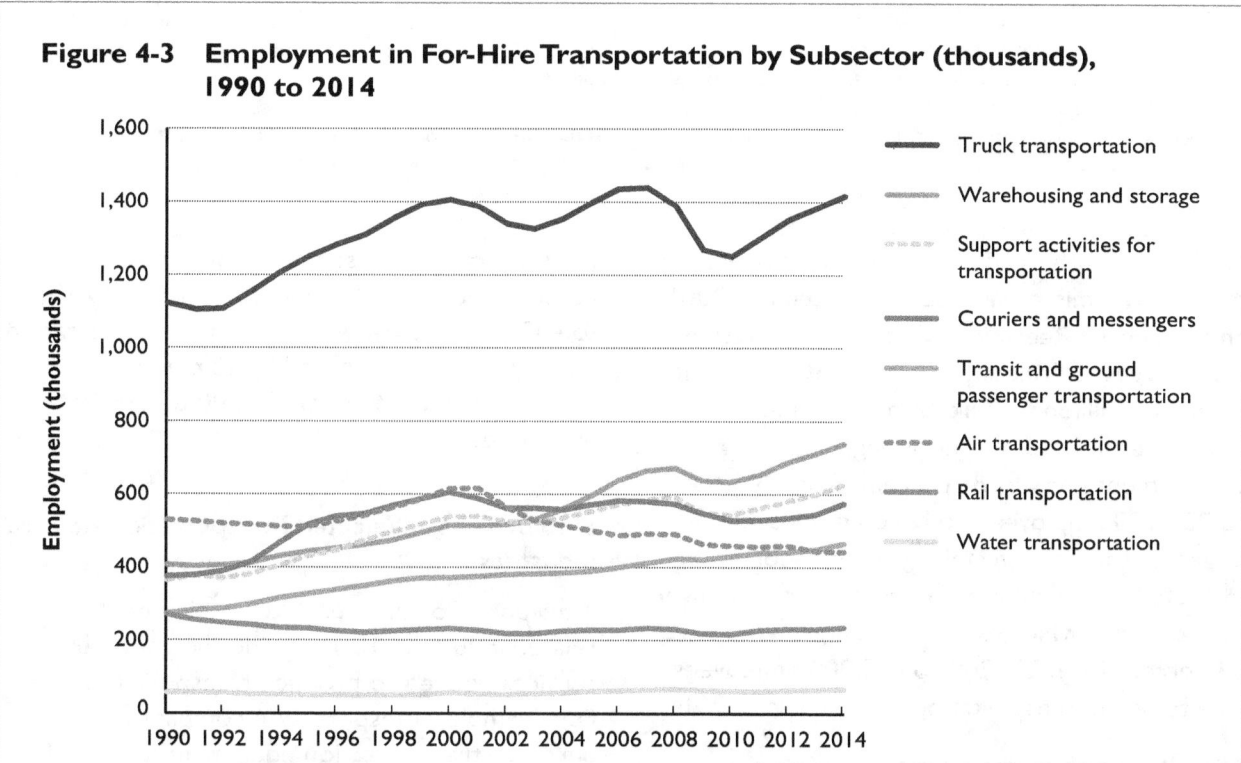

SOURCE: U.S. Department of Transportation, Bureau of Transportation Statistics, National Transportation Statistics, Table 3-23, available at www.bts.gov as of July 2016.

Box 4-3   Employment in the Transportation and Warehousing Sector

The **transportation and warehousing** sector (North American Industrial Classification System (NAICS) 48) includes air transportation, water transportation, truck transportation, transit and ground passenger transportation, pipeline transportation, scenic and sightseeing transportation, support activities for transportation (e.g., air traffic control and marine cargo handling), postal service, couriers and messengers, and warehousing and storage. It does not include government, railroad transportation, or self-employed persons.

Air transportation (NAICS 481) includes industries providing air transportation of passengers and cargo using aircraft, such as airplanes and helicopters. It does not include scenic and sightseeing air transportation, support activities for air transportation, or air courier services.

Water transportation (NAICS 483) includes industries providing water transportation of passengers and cargo using water craft, such as ships, barges, and boats. It does not include scenic and sightseeing water transportation services or support activities for water transportation.

Truck transportation (NAICS 484) includes industries providing over-the-road transportation of cargo using motor vehicles, such as trucks and tractor trailers. It does not include support activities for road transportation, freight transportation arrangement services, the Postal Service, or courier services.

Transit and ground passenger transportation (NAICS 485) includes industries providing a variety of passenger transportation activities, such as urban transit systems; chartered bus, school bus, and interurban bus transportation; and taxis. It does not include scenic and sightseeing transportation, support activities for road transportation, or arrangement for car pools and vanpools.

Pipeline transportation (NAICS 486) includes industries using transmission pipelines to transport products, such as crude oil, natural gas, refined petroleum products, and slurry. It does not include activities classified as utilities, such as natural gas distribution or water and air distribution and collection.

SOURCE: Bureau of Transportation Statistics, 2016.

employees, with significant fluctuations related to major economic events such as September 2001 and the Great Recession. Truck transportation is the largest subsector, employing 30.5 percent of the 4.6 million for-hire transportation employees in 2014. Warehousing and storage employment grew by 81 percent, from 406,600 to 738,000 employees, to become the second-largest subsector, overtaking air transportation in 1990. Meanwhile, transit and ground passenger employment, which experienced a growth rate of 69 percent from 274,200 to 465,000 employees, overtook air transportation at the close of 2014.

Not all for-hire transportation subsectors experienced employment increases from 1990 to 2014. For example, employment for couriers and messengers grew from 375,000 to 605,000 employees in the 1990s, but had decreased to 574,000 employees by 2014—most likely because some of their functions have been replaced by email and other telecommunications. Similarly, employment in air transportation increased from 1995 to 2001, but declined afterward, leading

to an overall decrease in employment of 16 percent between 1990 and 2014, from 529,200 to 442,100 employees. Finally, rail transportation employment also declined by 13 percent from 1990 to 2014, from 271,800 to 235,000 employees.

Employment in Selected Transportation-Related Industries

Transportation also leads to employment in related industries that provide the goods and services needed to produce transportation. For example, transportation companies purchase transportation equipment (as do other companies engaged in in-house transportation), motor vehicle dealers and gas stations provide services that support household and business transportation, and a significant portion of the output of the petroleum industry is used for transportation.

Figure 4-4 shows trends in employment for selected transportation-related industries from 1990 to 2014. These industries include

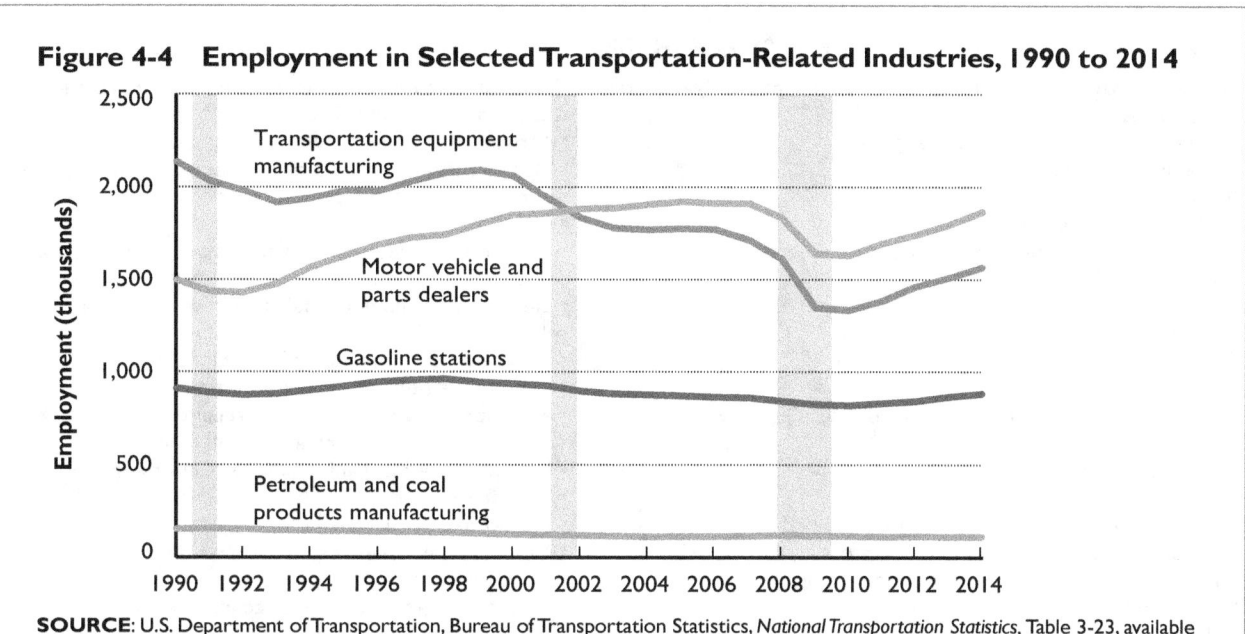

Figure 4-4   Employment in Selected Transportation-Related Industries, 1990 to 2014

SOURCE: U.S. Department of Transportation, Bureau of Transportation Statistics, *National Transportation Statistics,* Table 3-23, available at www.bts.gov as of July 2016.

motor vehicle and parts dealers, transportation equipment manufacturing, gasoline stations, and petroleum and coal products manufacturing. A notable shift in transportation-related employment occurred during this period. From 1990 to 2002, transportation equipment manufacturing was the largest transportation-related industry. However, as employment in transportation equipment manufacturing experienced a prolonged decline, motor vehicle and parts dealers became the largest industry in 2002. Employment in motor vehicle and parts dealers grew by 24.6 percent from 1990 to 2014.

Transportation Employment by Occupation

Many workers in transportation-related jobs are not included in employment data for transportation industries because they work for non-transportation firms. Table 4-1 highlights the enormous variety of positions available in various industries using the Standard Occupational Classification (SOC) system. Understanding the full range of transportation jobs and skills in the economy requires examination of employment data at the occupational level.

Table 4-2 lists the annual number of transportation and transportation-related jobs by occupation from 2007 to 2015. This table is derived from occupational employment and wage estimates produced by the Bureau of Labor Statistics for the Occupational Employment Statistics (OES) program (box 4-4). Table 4-2 also includes sparkline charts showing trends in employment for each occupation. The red dot on each line shows the lowest point, while the blue dot shows the highest point.

The largest transportation-related occupation is heavy-duty truck drivers; in 2015, 1.7 million people worked as heavy-duty truck drivers. Four of the six largest transportation-related occupations in 2014 involve driving and account for 38 percent of total employment:

- Heavy-duty truck drivers (1,678,280 million employees)

45

Table 4-1   Transportation-Related Occupations

Vehicle operators, pipeline operators, and primary support occupations
- Airline pilots, copilots, and flight engineers
- Commercial pilots
- Air traffic controllers
- Airfield operations specialists
- Ambulance drivers and attendants, except emergency medical technicians
- Bus drivers, transit and intercity
- Bus drivers, school
- Driver/sales workers
- Truck drivers, heavy and tractor-trailer
- Truck drivers, light or delivery services
- Taxi drivers and chauffeurs
- Locomotive engineers
- Locomotive firers
- Rail yard engineers, dinkey operators, and hostlers
- Railroad brake, signal, and switch operators
- Railroad conductors and yardmasters
- Subway and street car operators
- Sailors and marine oilers
- Captains, mates, and pilots of water vessels
- Motorboat operators
- Ship engineers
- Bridge and lock tenders
- Gas compressor and gas pumping station operators
- Pump operators, except wellhead pumpers

Secondary support service occupations
- Insurance appraisers, auto damage
- Parking enforcement workers
- Transit and railroad police
- Crossing guards
- Travel guides
- Flight attendants
- Transportation attendants, except flight attendants and baggage porters
- Travel agents
- Reservation and transportation ticket agents and travel clerks
- Couriers and messengers
- Dispatchers, except police, fire, and ambulance
- Postal service mail carriers
- Shipping, receiving, and traffic clerks
- Parking lot attendants
- Traffic technicians
- Transportation inspectors
- Refuse and recyclable material collectors
- Tank car, truck, and ship loaders

Transportation equipment manufacturing and maintenance occupations
- Aerospace engineers
- Marine engineers and naval architects
- Aerospace engineering and operations technicians
- Avionics technicians
- Electrical and electronics installers and repairers, transportation equipment
- Electronic equipment installers and repairers, motor vehicles
- Aircraft mechanics and service technicians
- Automotive body and related repairers
- Automotive glass installers and repairers
- Automotive service technicians and mechanics
- Bus and truck mechanics and diesel engine specialists
- Rail car repairers
- Motorboat mechanics
- Motorcycle mechanics
- Bicycle repairers
- Recreational vehicle service technicians
- Tire repairers and changers
- Aircraft structure, surfaces, rigging, and systems assemblers
- Painters, transportation equipment
- Tire builders
- Automotive and watercraft service attendants
- Cleaners of vehicles and equipment

Transportation infrastructure construction and maintenance occupations
- Paving, surfacing, and tamping equipment operators
- Highway maintenance workers
- Rail-track laying and maintenance equipment operators
- Signal and track switch repairers
- Dredge operators

Other occupations
- Transportation, storage, and distribution managers
- Aircraft cargo handling supervisors
- First-line supervisors/managers of helpers, laborers, and material movers, hand
- First-line supervisors/managers of transportation and material-moving machine and vehicle operators

SOURCE: U.S. Department of Transportation, Bureau of Transportation Statistics, *National Transportation Statistics*, Table 3-24, available at www.bts.gov as of July 2016.

Table 4-2 Employment in Transportation and Transportation-Related Occupations, 2007 to 2014

Occupation	2007	2007–2015 trend	2015
All transportation occupations	9,148,550		8,927,340
Vehicle operators, pipeline operators, and primary support			
Airline pilots, copilots, and flight engineers	78,250		81,350
Commercial pilots	29,180		39,760
Bus drivers, transit and intercity	189,050		168,620
Bus drivers, school	461,590		505,560
Driver/sales workers	382,360		417,660
Truck drivers, heavy and tractor-trailer	1,693,590		1,678,280
Truck drivers, light or delivery services	922,900		826,510
Taxi drivers and chauffeurs	165,590		180,960
Locomotive engineers	41,760		37,490
Railroad conductors and yardmasters	37,540		42,330
Transportation equipment manufacturing and maintenance			
Aerospace engineers	85,510		66,980
Aircraft mechanics and service technicians	118,780		124,040
Automotive body and related repairers	152,790		143,040
Automotive service technicians and mechanics	650,780		638,080
Bus and truck mechanics and diesel engine specialists	250,370		251,750
Tire repairers and changers	100,510		107,500
Aircraft structure, surfaces, rigging, and systems assemblers	34,410		42,810
Painters, transportation equipment	51,260		51,760
Automotive and watercraft service attendants	93,140		109,710
Cleaners of vehicles and equipment	336,210		336,960
Transportation infrastructure construction and maintenance occupations			
Paving, surfacing, and tamping equipment operators	63,850		53,110
Highway maintenance workers	137,140		142,300

NOTES: Occupations within the SOC's Transportation and Material Moving Occupations group are aggregated by subgroup. Blue dots on the sparkline charts indicate high values; red dots indicate low values.

SOURCE: U.S. Department of Transportation, Bureau of Transportation Statistics, *National Transportation Statistics*, Table 3-24, available at www.bts.gov as of July 2016.

Box 4-4   Occupational Employment Statistics

The Bureau of Labor Statistics (BLS) produces annual occupational employment and wage estimates as part of the Occupational Employment Statistics (OES) program. BLS conducts a semiannual survey of establishments to produce estimates for over 800 industries in the United States. The survey covers all full-time and part-time paid workers in non-farm industries, but does not include self-employed or unpaid workers.

The transportation occupations in table 4-1 and 4-2 cover the following worker types:

- Workers directly employed by a transportation company

- Workers engaged in in-house transportation

- Workers providing services to the transportation industry

- Workers providing transportation for non-transportation government agencies such as school districts

The occupations were selected based on a broad definition of transportation and transportation-related occupations found in Sen, B. and M. Rossetti, "A Complete Count of the U.S. Transportation Workforce," *Transportation Research Record* 1719: 2000, pp 259-266.

SOURCE: Bureau of Transportation Statistics, 2016.

- Light-duty and delivery truck drivers (826,510 employees)

- School bus drivers (505,560 employees)

- Driver/sales workers (417,660 employees)

Data by occupation over time show the changing face of transportation employment. For example, there has been a steady increase in employment for subway and street car operators, corresponding with the increase employment for the transit and ground passenger transportation industry.

From 1990 to 2015, employment in transportation and transportation-related occupations decreased by 2.3 percent. Some of the declines in employment are likely due to the December 2007 to June 2009 recession, but other declines in employment—for example, declines for postal service mail carriers and for couriers and messengers—portend structural changes in transportation employment.

Many employees of transportation companies, such as accountants and computer programmers, work in occupations that are not considered transportation occupations. Conversely, many workers in transportation occupations are employed in other industries, such as truck drivers working for retail chains. Figure 4-5 illustrates this difference. While total employment in the transportation and warehousing sector and total employment in transportation occupations measure the role of transportation in employment, they are different measures and may not move in tandem.

Part-Time and Full-Time Employment in Transportation-Related Occupations

Transportation-related occupations employ a slightly lower percentage of part-time workers than average (figure 4-6). The percentage of part-time workers in transportation-related occupations increased from 22 percent to 27 percent from 2008 to 2009 due to the recession, but has decreased to 23 percent in 2015.

Wages and Compensation for Transportation-Related Occupations

Figure 4-7 compares compensation for workers in transportation-related occupations and workers in all occupations from 2004 to 2016. Compensation includes wages and benefits. In current dollars, compensation for workers in transportation-related occupations increased 41 percent since 2004, to $27.89 in the first quarter of 2016. In comparison, wages for all occupations increased 36 percent to $33.94. Low-wage transportation occupations, like truck drivers and household movers, account for a much larger share of the transportation workforce than high-

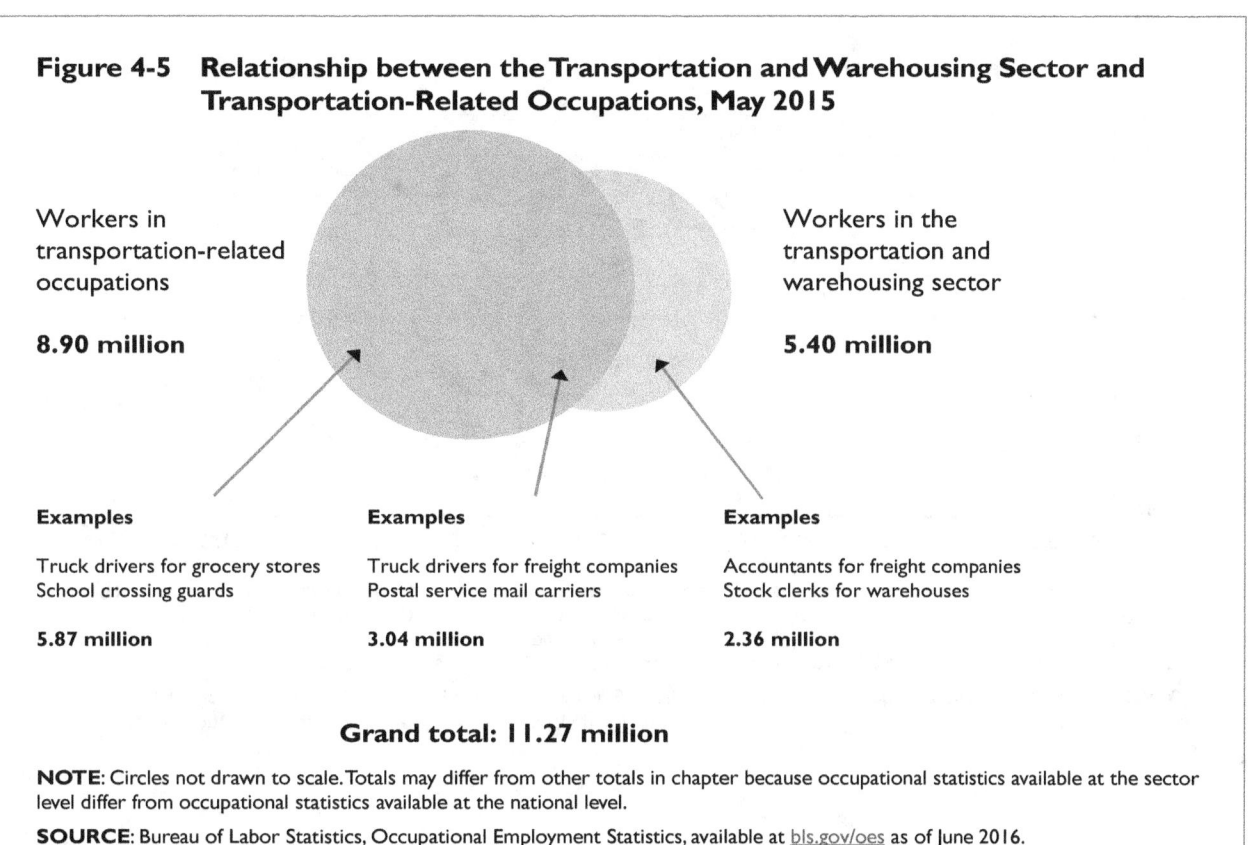

Figure 4-5   Relationship between the Transportation and Warehousing Sector and Transportation-Related Occupations, May 2015

Workers in transportation-related occupations

8.90 million

Workers in the transportation and warehousing sector

5.40 million

Examples

Truck drivers for grocery stores
School crossing guards

5.87 million

Examples

Truck drivers for freight companies
Postal service mail carriers

3.04 million

Examples

Accountants for freight companies
Stock clerks for warehouses

2.36 million

Grand total: 11.27 million

NOTE: Circles not drawn to scale. Totals may differ from other totals in chapter because occupational statistics available at the sector level differ from occupational statistics available at the national level.

SOURCE: Bureau of Labor Statistics, Occupational Employment Statistics, available at bls.gov/oes as of June 2016.

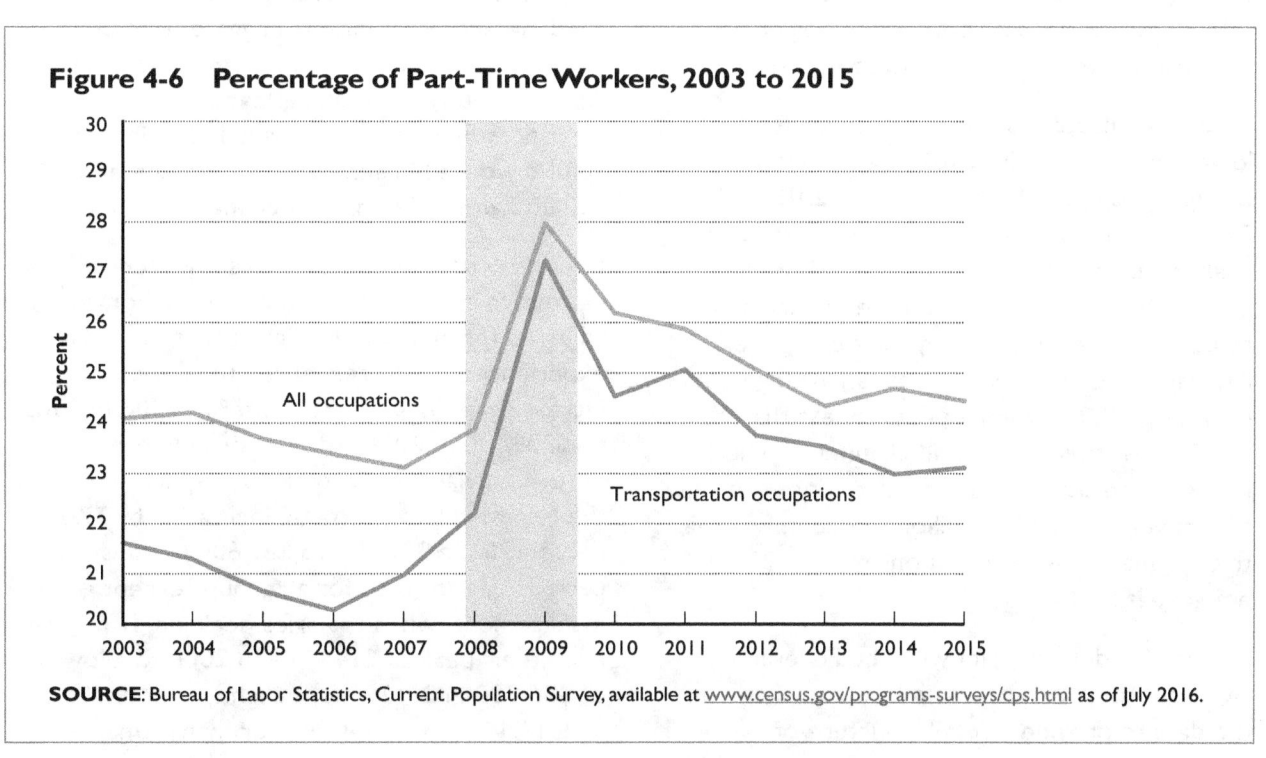

Figure 4-6   Percentage of Part-Time Workers, 2003 to 2015

All occupations

Transportation occupations

SOURCE: Bureau of Labor Statistics, Current Population Survey, available at www.census.gov/programs-surveys/cps.html as of July 2016.

Figure 4-7   Average Hourly Compensation (Wages and Benefits), 2004 to 2016

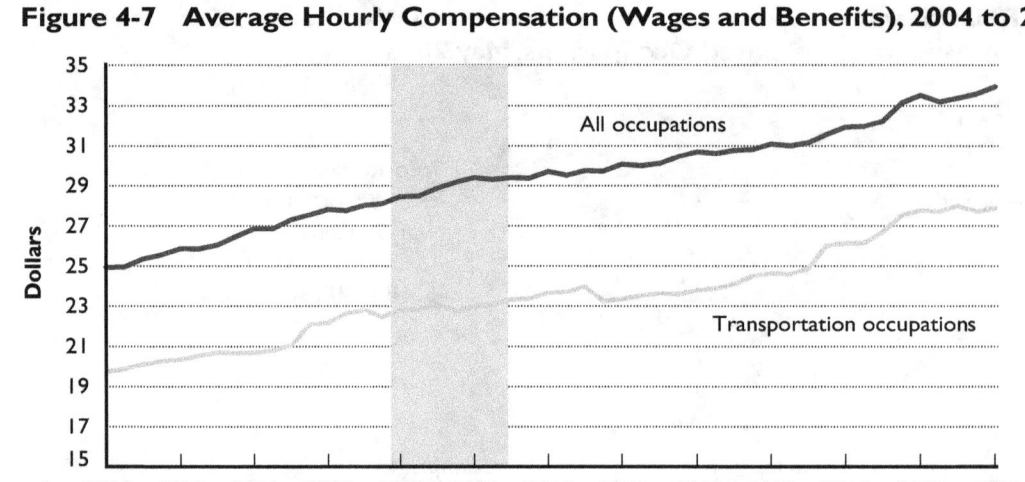

NOTES: The Bureau of Labor Statistics conducts the National Compensation Survey which provides quarterly data measuring level of average costs per hour worked. NCS is a survey of employers, which gathers data on both wages and benefits, including health insurance, pensions and paid leave. It is used to generate data on benefits, and to estimate the Employment Cost Index, which is used as an indicator by the Federal Reserve Board, as well as to generate data on changes in employer costs.

SOURCES: U.S. Department of Labor, Bureau of Labor Statistics, Employer Costs for Employee Compensation for Total Civilian compensation for All occupations and Total Civilian compensation for Transportation and material moving occupations, available at www.bls.gov/ncs/ect/#tables.

wage occupations like airline pilots. As a result, the average compensation for transportation-related occupations is about 6 dollars per hour less than the average for all occupations.

Figure 4-8 illustrates annual wages for the largest, lowest-paid, and highest-paid transportation occupations in the United States in 2015. Because some occupations are more seasonal, analysts use annual wage data instead of the average hourly compensation used in figure 4-7 to compare industry employment categories. Annual wages vary widely, from an average of over $100,000 for airline pilots to less than $25,000 for taxi drivers and chauffeurs. The 5 lowest-wage transportation-related occupations collectively employ 1.2 million workers, whereas the 5 highest-wage occupations employ 288,270 employees.

Airlines file detailed data with the Federal Aviation Administration, and BTS compiles the data to provide a detailed picture of

airline labor. In 2014, approximately 260,000 employees worked in aircraft and traffic handling—for example, as baggage handlers, as flight dispatchers, or as reservations clerks. Approximately 80,000 employees worked as in-flight personnel, 50,000 worked in maintenance, 10,000 worked in general management, and 160,000 worked in other occupations.

Figure 4-9 uses airline data to show trends in average annual salaries for airline labor, adjusted for inflation. In-flight personnel salaries experienced the largest absolute growth, increasing by 32 percent, from $158,200 in 2005 to $209,100 in 2014. Salaries for employees in "other aviation occupations" experienced the largest relative growth, increasing by 77.4 percent, from $21,200 to $37,600 in the same period. Salaries rose for all groups except general management, whose salaries declined 41 percent from their peak of $144,784 in 2006 to a low of $86,000 in 2012 before slightly rebounding in 2013. Moreover, salaries for management

Figure 4-8 Employment and Wages for Select Transportation Occupations, 2015

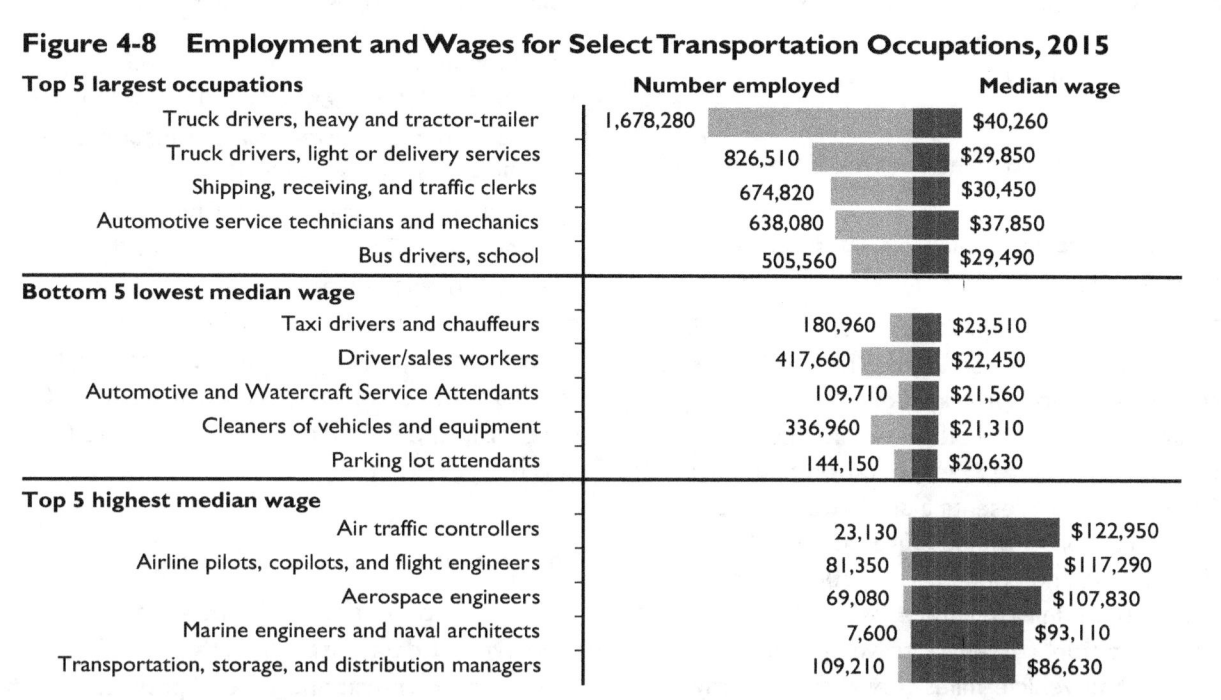

Top 5 largest occupations	Number employed	Median wage
Truck drivers, heavy and tractor-trailer	1,678,280	$40,260
Truck drivers, light or delivery services	826,510	$29,850
Shipping, receiving, and traffic clerks	674,820	$30,450
Automotive service technicians and mechanics	638,080	$37,850
Bus drivers, school	505,560	$29,490
Bottom 5 lowest median wage		
Taxi drivers and chauffeurs	180,960	$23,510
Driver/sales workers	417,660	$22,450
Automotive and Watercraft Service Attendants	109,710	$21,560
Cleaners of vehicles and equipment	336,960	$21,310
Parking lot attendants	144,150	$20,630
Top 5 highest median wage		
Air traffic controllers	23,130	$122,950
Airline pilots, copilots, and flight engineers	81,350	$117,290
Aerospace engineers	69,080	$107,830
Marine engineers and naval architects	7,600	$93,110
Transportation, storage, and distribution managers	109,210	$86,630

SOURCES: U.S. Department of Labor, Bureau of Labor Statistics, Occupational Employment and Wages, available at www.bls.gov/oes as of August 2016.

Figure 4-9 Average Annual Salary by Aviation Occupation (current dollars)

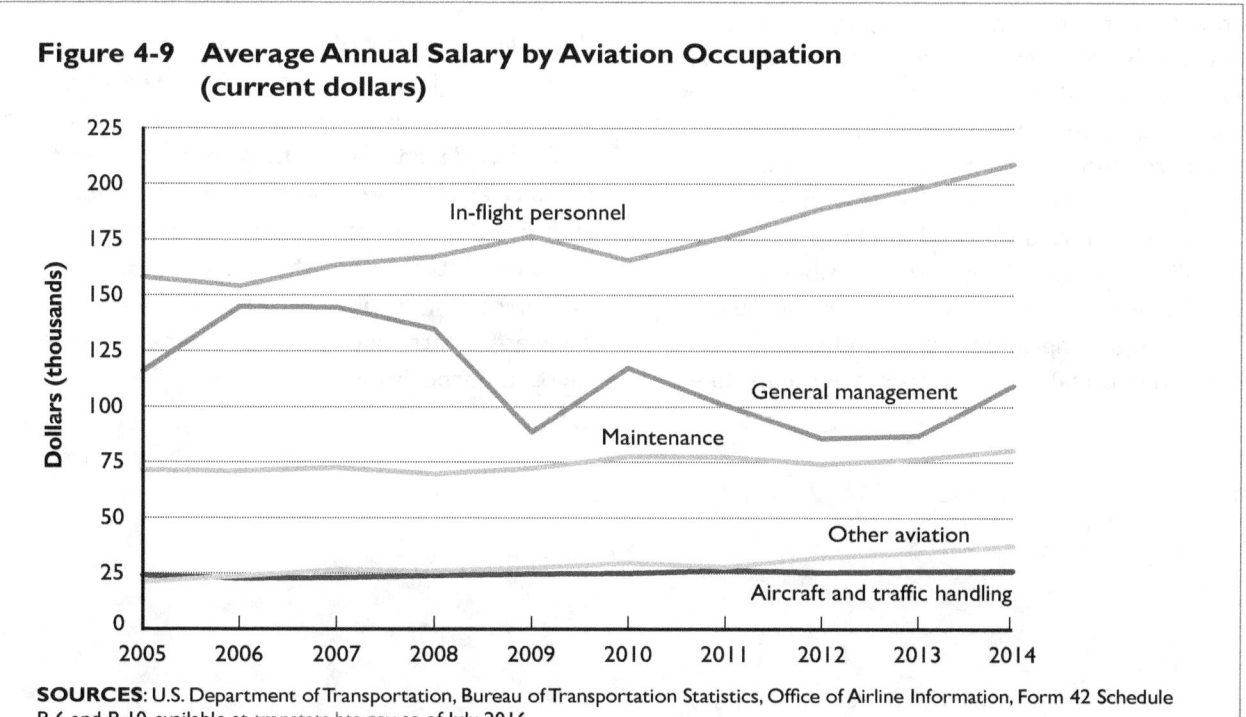

SOURCES: U.S. Department of Transportation, Bureau of Transportation Statistics, Office of Airline Information, Form 42 Schedule P-6 and P-10, available at transtats.bts.gov as of July 2016.

declined precipitously from 2008 to 2009; this decline may be related to structural changes in the airline industry.

Transportation Employment by State

Transportation Establishments, Employees, and Payroll

Transportation establishments employ people throughout the United States. To highlight state-by-state variations in transportation, including variations in transportation employment, BTS publishes State Transportation Statistics (STS). The STS presents a statistical profile of transportation in the 50 states and the District of Columbia and contains over 100 tables of state data on infrastructure, safety, freight transportation, passenger travel, registered vehicles and vehicle-miles traveled, economy and finance, and energy and environment.

Table 4-3 shows information about transportation establishments, employees, and total employee payroll for each state; figure 4-10 shows the relative share of employees in each state. Self-employed workers, freight railroad employees, and government employees are not included. State transportation employment is highly related to population and locations of transportation hubs. The five most populated states—California, Texas, Florida, New York, and Illinois—have the greatest number of establishments and employees, both because they have a large employment pool and because they contain national large transportation hubs like

railroad interchanges or major ports.

Transportation establishments collectively account for 3.7 percent of total payroll in the United States. However, many transportation establishments are small businesses, as shown by the national average establishment size of 20 employees. Transportation establishments employ anywhere from 0.6 percent of total state employees in the District of Columbia to 7.5 percent of employees in Alaska. Accordingly, the share of total state payroll ranges from 0.4 percent in the District of Columbia to 10.0 percent in Alaska.

Employment by Mode

Tables 4-4 to 4-9 provide transportation employment data for each state by mode (air, water, truck, transit and ground passenger, and freight railroad), and figure 4-11 illustrates the state distribution of modal employment. While transportation employment remains related to population, there is some variation by mode. For example, Texas, Louisiana, and Oklahoma have the largest number of pipeline establishments, even though Louisiana and Oklahoma are the 25th and 28th most populated states. In contrast, while Florida is the third most populated state, it has relatively few pipeline establishments and ranks 27th among states. For freight railroad, Nebraska has the third-largest number of employees, despite being the 37th most populated state, due to the presence of a major railroad corporation.

Table 4-3 Transportation Establishments, Employment, and Payroll by State, 2013

State	Transportation establishments	Paid employees	Percent of total employees in state	Average employees per establishment	Annual payroll ($ thousands)	Percent of total payroll in state
Alabama	2,845	58,471	3.70	21	2,490,950	4.20
Alaska	1,084	19,097	7.50	18	1,345,399	10.00
Arizona	3,161	81,274	3.90	26	3,693,380	4.30
Arkansas	2,364	49,665	5.10	21	2,159,077	6.10
California	21,397	445,742	3.50	21	20,797,494	3.10
Colorado	3,457	63,219	3.20	18	3,086,311	3.30
Connecticut	1,611	40,491	2.80	25	1,729,350	2.10
Delaware	637	11,804	3.30	19	486,891	2.80
District of Columbia	157	2,845	0.60	18	141,502	0.40
Florida	13,517	209,498	3.10	15	9,223,123	3.50
Georgia	6,102	164,898	5.00	27	7,549,952	5.30
Hawaii	851	27,868	5.70	33	1,239,320	6.70
Idaho	1,735	16,858	3.50	10	610,622	3.60
Illinois	13,636	225,959	4.50	17	10,274,004	4.20
Indiana	5,082	122,587	5.00	24	4,753,813	5.00
Iowa	3,485	55,443	4.40	16	2,129,910	4.60
Kansas	2,492	49,763	4.50	20	2,006,261	4.60
Kentucky	2,826	83,574	5.70	30	3,998,594	7.40
Louisiana	3,830	69,766	4.30	18	3,876,909	5.90
Maine	1,195	14,649	3.10	12	574,154	3.20
Maryland	3,393	64,301	3.10	19	2,747,431	2.70
Massachusetts	3,553	77,211	2.60	22	3,371,837	2.00
Michigan	5,734	100,454	3.00	18	4,720,501	3.20
Minnesota	4,620	77,561	3.20	17	3,271,392	3.00
Mississippi	2,030	33,202	3.70	16	1,356,791	4.60
Missouri	4,479	81,996	3.60	18	3,291,794	3.60
Montana	1,434	12,387	3.70	9	501,434	4.40
Nebraska	2,293	27,758	3.50	12	1,164,097	3.90
Nevada	1,403	46,119	4.60	33	1,789,598	4.60
New Hampshire	804	12,309	2.20	15	465,939	1.90
New Jersey	7,171	158,946	4.70	22	7,746,426	4.20
New Mexico	1,389	17,620	2.90	13	748,953	3.40
New York	12,364	233,149	3.20	19	10,107,169	2.30
North Carolina	5,407	107,649	3.30	20	4,507,539	3.40
North Dakota	1,683	18,846	6.20	11	1,100,936	9.00
Ohio	7,000	158,169	3.60	23	6,928,667	3.80
Oklahoma	2,685	46,789	3.70	17	2,341,925	4.70
Oregon	2,940	50,836	3.80	17	2,215,373	3.90
Pennsylvania	8,227	206,938	4.10	25	8,240,126	3.70
Rhode Island	609	10,103	2.50	17	376,680	2.20
South Carolina	2,472	52,756	3.50	21	2,144,466	3.90
South Dakota	1,185	9,686	3.00	8	381,443	3.40
Tennessee	3,988	125,010	5.40	31	5,403,271	5.90
Texas	17,501	390,221	4.30	22	20,622,776	5.00
Utah	2,205	47,856	4.70	22	2,124,148	5.30
Vermont	489	6,266	2.40	13	222,453	2.30
Virginia	4,801	95,463	3.20	20	4,307,669	3.00
Washington	4,883	86,375	3.70	18	4,453,992	3.80
West Virginia	1,205	13,857	2.40	11	592,686	2.90
Wisconsin	5,171	93,997	4.00	18	3,747,073	3.90
Wyoming	965	9,935	4.80	10	495,120	5.40
United States, total	**215,547**	**4,287,236**	**3.80**	**20**	**193,656,721**	**3.70**

SOURCE: U.S. Department of Transportation, Bureau of Transportation Statistics, *State Transportation Statistics*, Table 6-1, available at www.bts. gov as of July 2016.

Figure 4-10   State Share of Transportation Employment

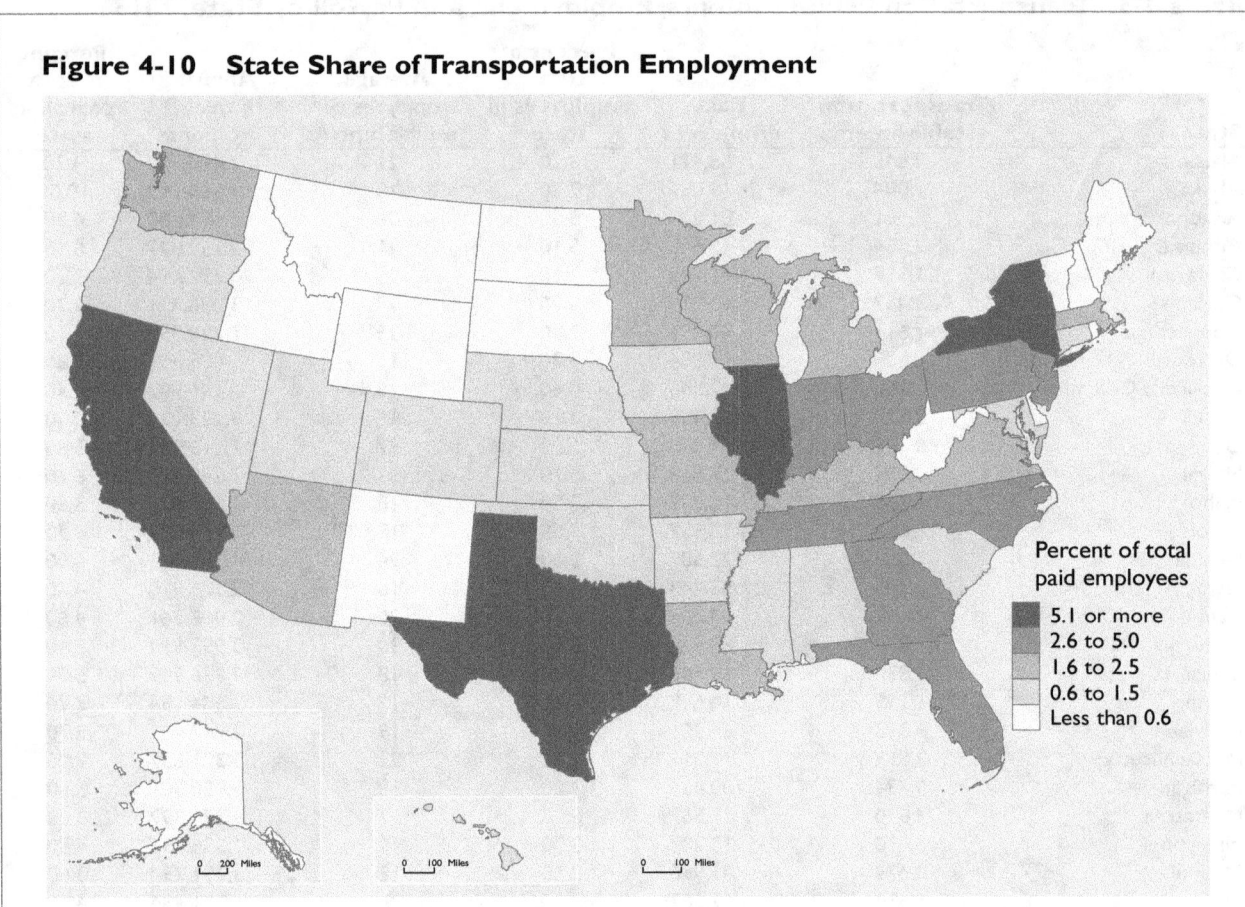

SOURCE: U.S. Department of Transportation, Bureau of Transportation Statistics, *State Transportation Statistics*, Table 6-1, available at www.bts.gov as of July 2016.

Table 4-4 Air Transportation Establishments, Employment, and Payroll by State, 2013

State	Number of establishments	Number of paid employees	Annual payroll ($ thousands)
Alabama	45	629	33,508
Alaska	196	5,773	315,963
Arizona	110	W	W
Arkansas	39	423	16,825
California	552	44,075	2,880,699
Colorado	103	15,614	907,706
Connecticut	42	1,400	83,677
Delaware	26	190	11,352
District of Columbia	15	W	W
Florida	533	22,099	1,266,728
Georgia	125	30,665	2,008,440
Hawaii	62	8,377	473,553
Idaho	49	1,082	47,841
Illinois	187	W	W
Indiana	71	W	126,704
Iowa	31	278	8,842
Kansas	34	406	16,300
Kentucky	49	4,191	247,294
Louisiana	103	4,654	277,909
Maine	20	184	5,458
Maryland	40	W	W
Massachusetts	87	7,683	410,361
Michigan	106	12,545	888,907
Minnesota	57	W	W
Mississippi	39	285	10,160
Missouri	62	W	W
Montana	64	779	33,929
Nebraska	30	577	31,424
Nevada	58	W	W
New Hampshire	25	W	W
New Jersey	101	14,846	1,281,137
New Mexico	38	611	31,855
New York	332	32,918	2,084,308
North Carolina	101	W	W
North Dakota	16	135	4,174
Ohio	102	10,906	877,901
Oklahoma	49	W	W
Oregon	80	5,242	333,669
Pennsylvania	124	W	W
Rhode Island	10	W	W
South Carolina	47	998	40,655
South Dakota	25	163	6,038
Tennessee	69	4,299	227,449
Texas	449	W	W
Utah	39	7,910	410,861
Vermont	7	91	3,053
Virginia	125	W	W
Washington	106	11,431	823,326
West Virginia	9	W	1,886
Wisconsin	51	1,381	51,099
Wyoming	24	W	W
United States, total	**4,864**	**418,936**	**26,921,123**

NOTE: "W" indicates data withheld to avoid disclosure.

SOURCE: U.S. Department of Transportation, Bureau of Transportation Statistics, *State Transportation Statistics 2015*, Table 6-2, available at www.bts.gov as of July 2016.

Table 4-5 Water Transportation Establishments, Employment, and Payroll by State, 2013

State	Number of establishments	Number of paid employees	Annual payroll ($ thousands)
Alabama	95	1,677	31,776
Alaska	74	1,633	36,683
Arizona	266	9,132	238,928
Arkansas	61	1,083	21032
California	2,083	43,539	1,257,956
Colorado	219	4,944	142,502
Connecticut	383	14,009	383,207
Delaware	135	1,894	29396
District of Columbia	45	1,119	38,291
Florida	1043	13,248	342,405
Georgia	332	5,187	128,732
Hawaii	111	4,526	162,884
Idaho	81	1,803	30,327
Illinois	1104	26,994	550,168
Indiana	236	11,457	169,245
Iowa	104	1,707	45,146
Kansas	144	8,302	132,248
Kentucky	110	1,984	43,596
Louisiana	180	3,812	103,655
Maine	92	1,458	26,385
Maryland	703	11,340	280,892
Massachusetts	807	23,457	718,763
Michigan	349	7,003	155,992
Minnesota	503	14,383	295,800
Mississippi	82	1,828	34,120
Missouri	301	9,010	172,062
Montana	89	1,319	19,674
Nebraska	70	1,842	28,045
Nevada	149	15,577	385,585
New Hampshire	122	3,689	73,897
New Jersey	1,038	29,055	694,391
New Mexico	131	3,691	67,300
New York	2,976	73,467	2,188,905
North Carolina	296	4,551	103,498
North Dakota	66	1,038	20419
Ohio	400	9,829	182,182
Oklahoma	92	1,433	26384
Oregon	249	4,937	96,300
Pennsylvania	1,140	35,200	642,005
Rhode Island	99	2,948	56,923
South Carolina	148	1,632	38,433
South Dakota	86	1,148	21,095
Tennessee	276	4,803	136,872
Texas	716	19,091	503,392
Utah	80	1,581	27,416
Vermont	61	1,439	28,584
Virginia	426	8,523	258,332
Washington	288	5,576	159,583
West Virginia	42	400	5,952
Wisconsin	492	13,832	243,014
Wyoming	23	267	6676
United States, total	**19,198**	**473,397**	**11,587,048**

NOTE: "W" indicates data withheld to avoid disclosure.

SOURCE: U.S. Department of Transportation, Bureau of Transportation Statistics, *State Transportation Statistics 2015*, Table 6-2, available at www. bts.gov as of July 2016.

Table 4-6 Truck Transportation Establishments, Employment, and Payroll by State, 2013

State	Number of establishments	Number of paid employees	Annual payroll ($ thousands)
Alabama	1,692	25,591	1,000,439
Alaska	228	3,071	169,662
Arizona	1,397	22,134	866,289
Arkansas	1,503	31,703	1,438,892
California	9,304	105,264	4,655,923
Colorado	1,911	19,875	937,482
Connecticut	571	5,717	293,298
Delaware	231	3,086	123,526
District of Columbia	14	106	4,789
Florida	5,244	45,730	1,860,840
Georgia	3,133	48,472	2,042,001
Hawaii	195	3,325	134,010
Idaho	1,223	9,811	371,260
Illinois	8,801	68,952	3,176,110
Indiana	3,353	53,874	2,298,505
Iowa	2,612	36,065	1,361,041
Kansas	1,569	19,325	842,120
Kentucky	1,656	21,151	883,363
Louisiana	1,653	17,928	750,524
Maine	699	5,428	211,147
Maryland	1,447	15,479	678,264
Massachusetts	1,353	15,763	749,918
Michigan	3,407	42,509	1,963,534
Minnesota	2,866	26,402	1,172,656
Mississippi	1,234	13,771	557,601
Missouri	2,714	37,296	1,548,015
Montana	909	6,348	286,224
Nebraska	1,716	14,624	614,711
Nevada	558	6,287	284,980
New Hampshire	396	3,449	147,365
New Jersey	3,259	38,200	1,815,635
New Mexico	753	7,606	374,207
New York	4,501	39,800	1,734,713
North Carolina	3,014	40,340	1,687,003
North Dakota	1,327	13,887	874,076
Ohio	4,110	59,256	2,680,696
Oklahoma	1,725	20,021	912,162
Oregon	1,560	18,316	770,317
Pennsylvania	4,428	60,941	2,799,016
Rhode Island	277	2,663	126,949
South Carolina	1,213	17,269	740,298
South Dakota	859	4,952	208,026
Tennessee	1,963	48,710	2,243,234
Texas	8,639	130,575	6,123,275
Utah	1,435	21,185	1,016,095
Vermont	297	2,918	108,990
Virginia	2,554	29,254	1,228,829
Washington	2,438	22,925	1,016,832
West Virginia	794	6,262	252,846
Wisconsin	3,458	48,066	2,162,852
Wyoming	656	4,952	254,515
United States, total	**112,849**	**1,366,634**	**60,555,055**

SOURCE: U.S. Department of Transportation, Bureau of Transportation Statistics, *State Transportation Statistics 2015*, Table 6-5, available at www.bts.gov as of July 2016.

Table 4-7 Transit and Ground Passenger Transportation Establishments, Employment, and Payroll by State, 2013

State	Number of establishments	Number of paid employees	Annual payroll ($ thousands)
Alabama	22	920	62,337
Alaska	78	W	98,156
Arizona	4	W	W
Arkansas	2	W	W
California	98	5,522	429,882
Colorado	2	W	W
Connecticut	29	966	85,969
Delaware	8	55	4,060
District of Columbia	W	W	W
Florida	214	14,667	939,639
Georgia	15	W	7,475
Hawaii	10	W	W
Idaho	1	W	W
Illinois	44	1,283	83,102
Indiana	8	W	W
Iowa	4	W	W
Kansas	1	W	W
Kentucky	23	2,234	139,188
Louisiana	263	11,958	948,669
Maine	12	52	2,102
Maryland	28	183	12,525
Massachusetts	36	445	45,441
Michigan	38	468	39,640
Minnesota	11	W	W
Mississippi	16	1,104	75,697
Missouri	11	504	29,451
Montana	W	W	W
Nebraska	W	W	W
Nevada	3	W	W
New Hampshire	1	W	W
New Jersey	63	887	62,710
New Mexico	5	W	W
New York	125	2,361	191,651
North Carolina	30	W	W
North Dakota	W	W	W
Ohio	18	W	W
Oklahoma	1	W	W
Oregon	16	W	W
Pennsylvania	34	1,176	60,852
Rhode Island	7	77	3,591
South Carolina	13	W	W
South Dakota	W	W	W
Tennessee	13	2,439	158,654
Texas	119	4,986	427,694
Utah	4	W	W
Vermont	4	W	W
Virginia	33	1,319	104,135
Washington	79	5,585	346,877
West Virginia	4	W	W
Wisconsin	5	W	3,888
Wyoming	1	W	W
United States, total	**1,556**	**66,672**	**4,737,874**

NOTE: "W" indicates data withheld to avoid disclosure.

SOURCE: U.S. Department of Transportation, Bureau of Transportation Statistics, *State Transportation Statistics 2015*, Table 6-5, available at www. bts.gov as of July 2016.

Table 4-8 Pipeline Transportation Establishments, Employment, and Payroll by State, 2013

State	Number of establishments	Number of paid employees	Annual payroll ($ thousands)
Alabama	69	W	97,520
Alaska	16	1,456	267,975
Arizona	50	W	W
Arkansas	60	W	W
California	106	W	W
Colorado	102	W	W
Connecticut	15	164	19,255
Delaware	2	W	W
District of Columbia	7	W	W
Florida	53	W	W
Georgia	66	W	W
Hawaii	1	W	W
Idaho	5	W	6,876
Illinois	124	W	W
Indiana	64	538	50,929
Iowa	59	442	38,090
Kansas	143	1,716	162,111
Kentucky	60	954	83,197
Louisiana	335	W	314,489
Maine	13	W	7,307
Maryland	14	W	9,786
Massachusetts	30	343	39,208
Michigan	82	606	61,020
Minnesota	71	645	61,447
Mississippi	118	W	90,501
Missouri	66	W	29,221
Montana	30	252	23,218
Nebraska	57	698	65,061
Nevada	7	W	6,210
New Hampshire	11	36	3,851
New Jersey	40	333	34,797
New Mexico	88	925	85,905
New York	76	W	143,492
North Carolina	33	284	25,251
North Dakota	46	684	60,361
Ohio	87	W	W
Oklahoma	167	2,300	230,693
Oregon	13	131	13,716
Pennsylvania	147	1,987	172,273
Rhode Island	3	W	W
South Carolina	20	172	16,019
South Dakota	16	122	11,972
Tennessee	77	W	W
Texas	812	18,182	2,624,906
Utah	21	W	W
Vermont	3	W	W
Virginia	58	W	32,213
Washington	28	331	32,942
West Virginia	80	W	W
Wisconsin	50	W	39,833
Wyoming	90	839	77,380
United States, total	**3,791**	**52,021**	**6,070,358**

NOTE: "W" indicates data withheld to avoid disclosure.

SOURCE: U.S. Department of Transportation, Bureau of Transportation Statistics, *State Transportation Statistics 2015*, Table 6-6, available at www.bts.gov as of July 2016.

Table 4-9: Railroad Transportation Employment and Wages by State, 2013

State	Number of employees	Wages ($ millions)
Alabama	3,711	387
Alaska	525	48
Arizona	2,854	322
Arkansas	3,390	365
California	8,877	997
Colorado	2,973	337
Connecticut	117	11
Delaware	196	20
District of Columbia	12	1
Florida	4,981	529
Georgia	7,178	748
Hawaii	0	0
Idaho	1,390	151
Illinois	13,152	1,482
Indiana	6,223	659
Iowa	3,746	411
Kansas	5,427	626
Kentucky	4,195	446
Louisiana	3,083	339
Maine	650	65
Maryland	1,535	165
Massachusetts	823	75
Michigan	3,194	350
Minnesota	4,566	517
Mississippi	1,833	211
Missouri	7,333	832
Montana	2,805	321
Nebraska	12,010	1,364
Nevada	676	75
New Hampshire	242	20
New Jersey	1,132	118
New Mexico	1,671	196
New York	3,487	361
North Carolina	2,434	252
North Dakota	2,026	213
Ohio	7,619	791
Oklahoma	1,991	225
Oregon	2,026	220
Pennsylvania	7,056	718
Rhode Island	61	6
South Carolina	1,749	184
South Dakota	869	102
Tennessee	4,274	463
Texas	16,826	1,908
Utah	1,659	179
Vermont	172	14
Virginia	5,737	593
Washington	3,967	463
West Virginia	2,861	303
Wisconsin	3,128	358
Wyoming	2,822	323
United States, total	**181,264**	**19,861**

SOURCE: U.S. Department of Transportation, Bureau of Transportation Statistics, *State Transportation Statistics 2015*, Table 6-7, available at www.bts.gov as of July 2016.

Figure 4-11   State Share of Industry Employment by Mode

Air Transportation Employment

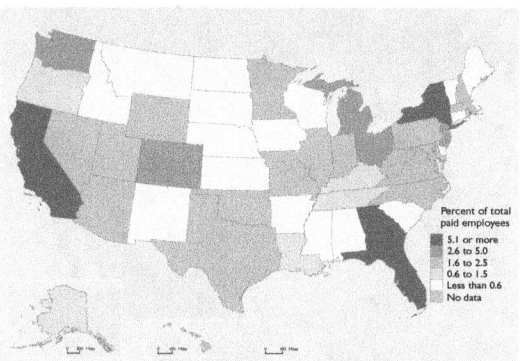

Water Transportation Employment

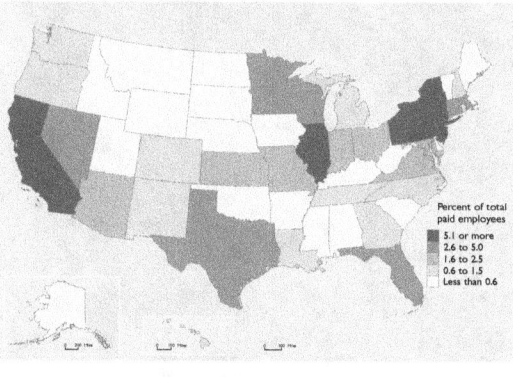

Truck Transportation Employment

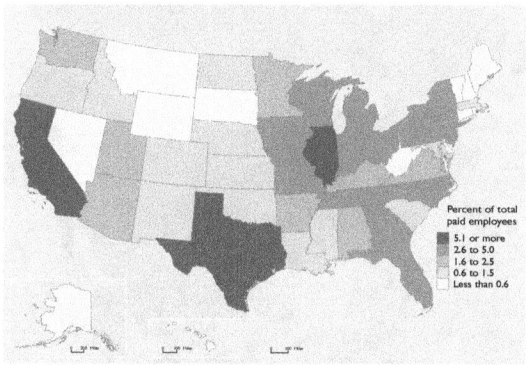

Transit and Ground Passenger Transportation Employment

Pipeline Transportation Employment

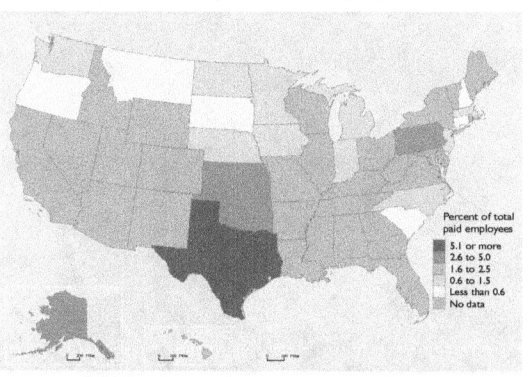

Freight Railroad Employment

SOURCES: U.S. Department of Transportation, Bureau of Transportation Statistics, *State Transportation Statistics 2015*, Tables 6-2 to 6-7, available at www.bts.gov as of February 2016.

5 TRANSPORTATION PRODUCTIVITY

What is Productivity?

In the general sense, "productivity" refers to the rate at which workers produce goods or complete work. *Economic productivity*, however, has a more precise definition: it is the ratio of total output to the inputs used in the production process. Inputs can include labor, capital, land, and entrepreneurship. If productivity increases, a business can produce the same output using fewer inputs. The business may then choose to produce more output, lower prices, invest in the business, or return income to shareholders.

Productivity for an industry can increase for a number of reasons. For example, new technology or training classes can allow workers to produce more goods in the same amount of time or with the same amount of resources. Likewise, policy changes can allow firms to operate more efficiently, such as when Congress deregulated railroads by passing the Staggers Rail Act of 1980, allowing railroads to abandon unprofitable routes and adopt labor-saving technologies.

Productivity growth is beneficial because increases in productivity improve economic wealth and the standard of living. One classic example is the Ford Motor Company's Model T automobile, produced in the early 1900s. Ford greatly increased productivity by using interchangeable parts and a moving assembly line. Ford chose to use the increased productivity to sell the Model T for a lower price than competing vehicles. As a result, more people could afford an automobile. Similarly, if a freight delivery company optimizes its routing and delivery schedules, it can offer lower prices to shippers.

As the freight delivery example suggests, transportation itself is an input for other industries. If the cost of providing transportation decreases, other industries become more productive as well, which reduces business costs and brings savings to consumers.

At the same time, however, many other factors besides productivity affect the performance of a firm or industry. For example, demand for a firm's products may decline even as the firm becomes more productive. In other words, productivity is necessary but not sufficient for economic well-being. Employment may also decrease in an industry as it becomes more productive. Automating certain processes may make a firm more productive, but may also lead to worker layoffs.

Productivity Measurements

Productivity measures provide answers to important questions about the transportation sector—for example, how efficiently transportation providers move people and goods, and whether the value of their services has grown more rapidly than the costs of the inputs they use. There are two main measures of transportation productivity: *labor (single-factor) productivity* and *multifactor productivity*. Labor productivity measures the output per unit of labor input, while multifactor productivity measures the output per unit as a weighted average of multiple factors, including fuel, equipment, and materials. While multifactor productivity is a more comprehensive measure of economic performance, labor productivity is easier to measure and continues to have a broad appeal.

In the United States, the Bureau of Labor Statistics (BLS) produces labor and multifactor productivity measures for industries as defined by the North American Industry Classification

System (NAICS).[1] These measures show industry changes in inputs, outputs, and productivity.

Labor Productivity

To measure *labor productivity*, BLS measures outputs by industry and divides the output by paid labor hours. When an industry has multiple products or services, the outputs are weighted by value. BLS indexes the ratios to a common base year to allow for comparisons over time. BLS measures allow comparisons among industries to analyze industry responses to regulations and policies, changes in labor costs, and competitive pressures.

Figure 5-1 illustrates changes in labor productivity for selected transportation industries from 1990 to 2015. Air transportation had the least productive labor force in 1990, but became the

---

[1] The Bureau of Economic Analysis also releases productivity measures. The BEA measures differ from the BLS measures because BEA calculates productivity using a gross-output approach, while the BLS uses a sectoral approach. Since 2002 the agencies have met to ensure that their estimates are compatible.

second most productive mode by 2015 after productivity increased by 158 percent. Railroads had the second least productive labor force in 1990, but became the most productive mode after productivity increased by 129 percent from 1990 to 2015. These large changes in air and rail labor productivity were spurred by deregulation, allowing for changes in labor requirements (e.g., reduced crew sizes) and changes in market competition. The labor force in long-distance freight trucking and the U.S. Postal Service (USPS) had smaller productivity increases of 33 and 15 percent, respectively. Moreover, the USPS moved from having the highest labor productivity in 1990 to having the lowest labor productivity in 2015.

Multifactor Productivity

To measure *multifactor productivity (MFP)*, BLS divides output by a weighted set of inputs, including labor hours, fuel, equipment, and materials. Changes in multifactor productivity reflect the combined effects of factors such as new technologies, new regulations, or organizational changes.

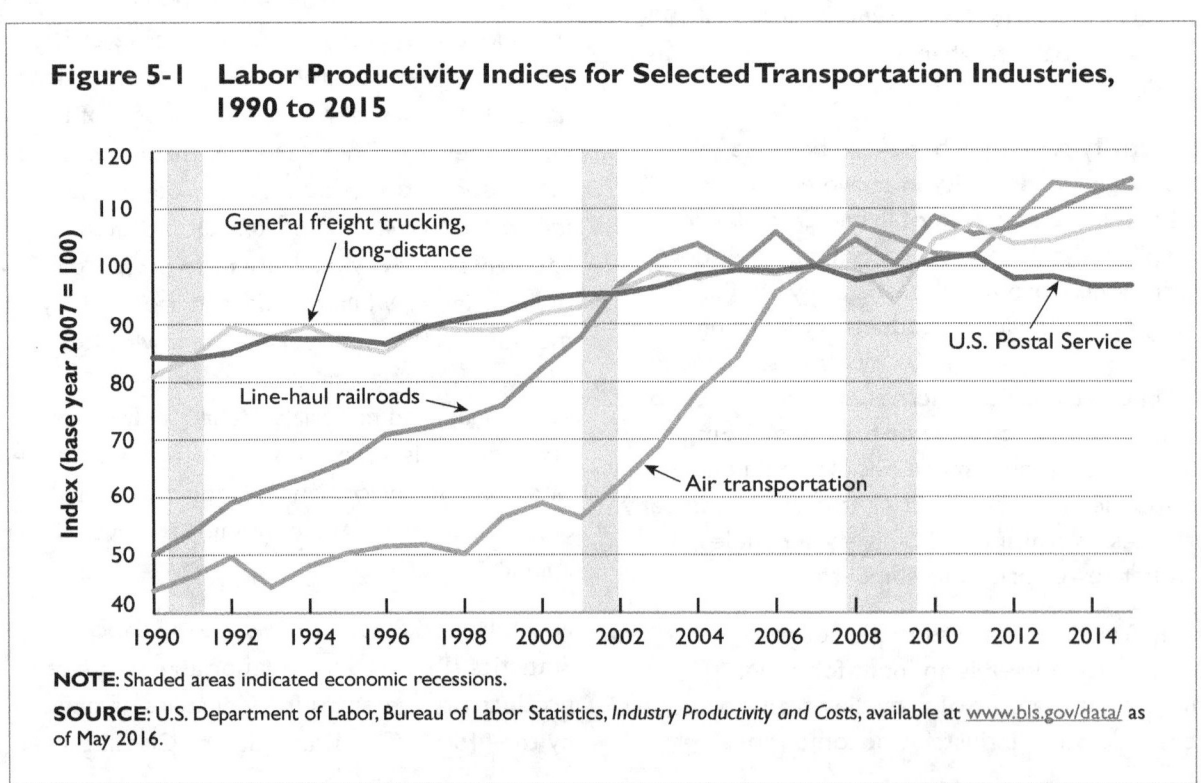

Figure 5-1   Labor Productivity Indices for Selected Transportation Industries, 1990 to 2015

NOTE: Shaded areas indicated economic recessions.

SOURCE: U.S. Department of Labor, Bureau of Labor Statistics, *Industry Productivity and Costs*, available at www.bls.gov/data/ as of May 2016.

From 1990 through 2013, air transportation and water transportation had the largest increases in MPF: 114 and 51 percent, respectively (Figure 5-2). MFP in air transportation was the lowest in 1990, but became the second highest by 2013. MFP in pipeline transportation had a smaller increase of 26 percent over the same period and showed considerably more year-to-year variation, but it remained the most productive industry in 2013 because of its relatively high productivity at the start of the period. Finally, MFP in the railroad industry increased 35 percent during the same period.

Per-Mile Revenue Measures

Another way to look at transportation productivity is to examine what users pay for transportation. This can be seen as an economic measure of the value of transportation. For passenger transportation, the unit of output is passenger-miles, and average revenue per passenger-mile is the measure of what travelers pay. For freight transportation, the unit of output is ton-miles, and average freight revenue per ton-mile is the measure of what freight shippers pay. For modes where users do not typically pay per use, like driving, complete data are difficult to obtain.

Revenue per Passenger-Mile

While nominal revenue per passenger-mile increased from 1990 to 2012, only Amtrak/intercity rail experienced real (inflation-adjusted) passenger revenue growth. Figure 5-3 shows nominal changes in revenue per passenger-mile from 1990 to 2013 relative to the index for all consumer expenditures (CPI) for three industries: domestic air carriers, commuter rail, and Amtrak/intercity rail. Intercity rail and Amtrak experienced the largest growth in revenue per passenger-mile, increasing 151 percent between 1990 and 2013, and commuter rail increased 70 percent. However, domestic air carrier revenue per passenger-mile remained almost unchanged, increasing 6 percent.

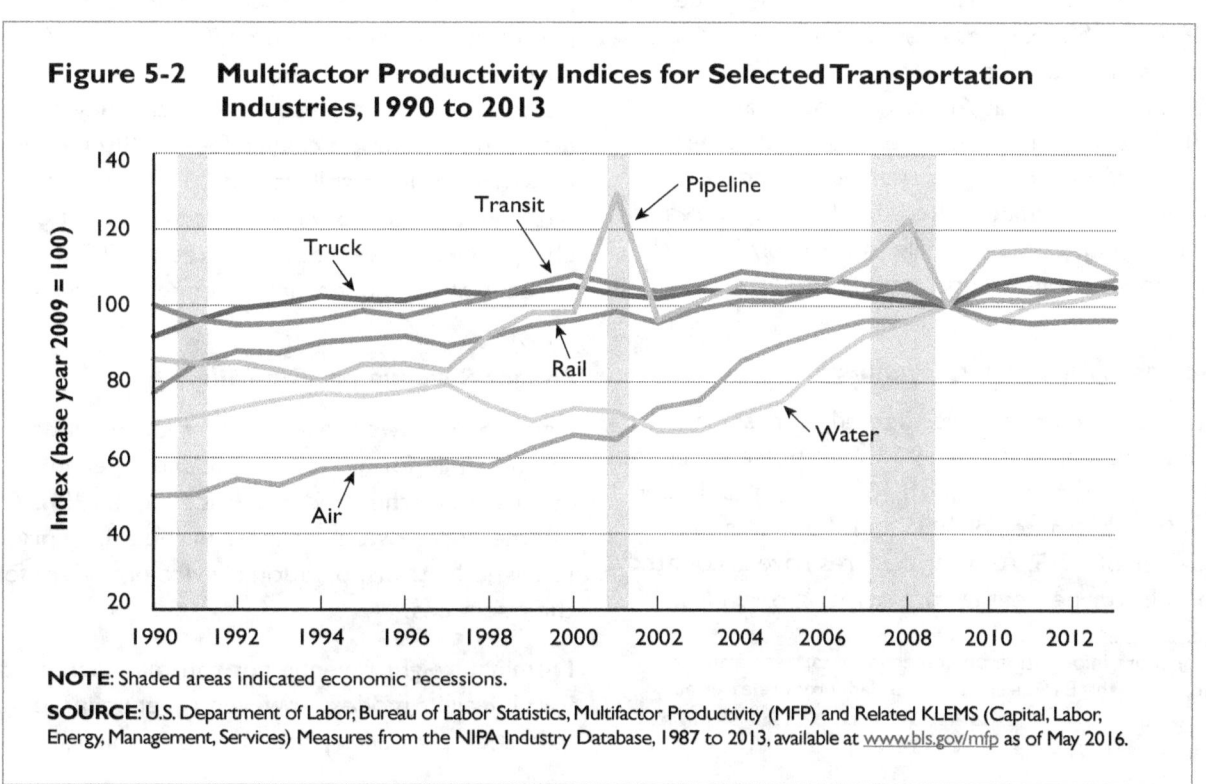

Figure 5-2   Multifactor Productivity Indices for Selected Transportation Industries, 1990 to 2013

NOTE: Shaded areas indicated economic recessions.

SOURCE: U.S. Department of Labor, Bureau of Labor Statistics, Multifactor Productivity (MFP) and Related KLEMS (Capital, Labor, Energy, Management, Services) Measures from the NIPA Industry Database, 1987 to 2013, available at www.bls.gov/mfp as of May 2016.

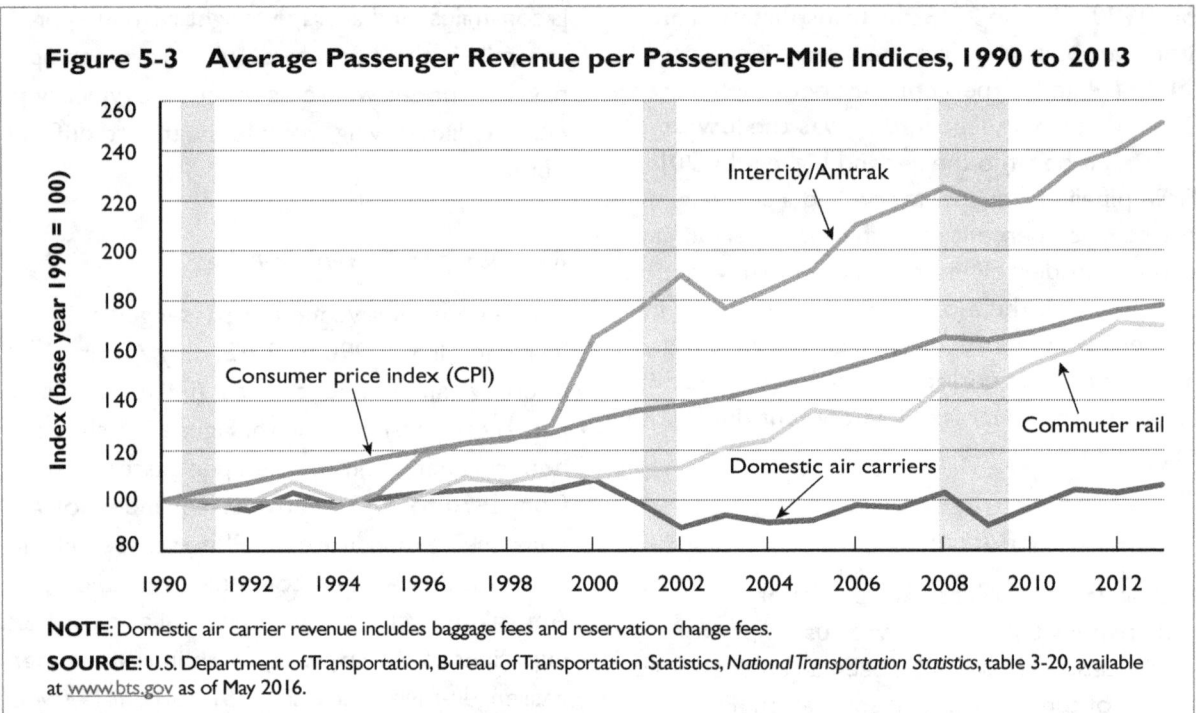

Figure 5-3 Average Passenger Revenue per Passenger-Mile Indices, 1990 to 2013

NOTE: Domestic air carrier revenue includes baggage fees and reservation change fees.

SOURCE: U.S. Department of Transportation, Bureau of Transportation Statistics, *National Transportation Statistics*, table 3-20, available at www.bts.gov as of May 2016.

The increases in revenue per passenger-mile are partly due to an increase in the overall price of goods and services. The Consumer Price Index (CPI), which measures overall changes in prices, increased by almost 80 percent from 1990 to 2013, indicating that Amtrak/intercity rail was the only industry with real increasing revenue per passenger-mile during the period. Domestic air carriers, meanwhile, suffered a decrease in real revenue per passenger-mile, most likely because of competitive pressures among air carriers.

Domestic Air Carrier Revenues

Two developments have affected domestic air carrier revenues from 1990 to the present.[2] First, domestic air fares declined 18.2 percent between the fourth quarter of 1995 and the fourth quarter of 2015. As a result, fares have accounted for a lower percentage of operating revenues.

---

[2] For more information on domestic air carrier revenues, please see the BTS airline financial data press releases at http://www.rita.dot.gov/bts/sites/rita.dot.gov.bts/files/press_releases/airline_financial_data.html.

In the 1990s, domestic air carriers received slightly below 90 percent of their revenues from passenger fares. In the 2000s, however, the percentage declined from 88.9 percent in 2000 to 73.7 percent in 2009, and has remained around 74 percent. Second, airlines began increasing baggage fees and reservation change fees in 2008. In 2015, passenger airlines collected $3.8 billion from baggage fees and $3.0 billion from reservation change fees; these fees accounted for 2.3 and 1.8 percent of total operating revenue, respectively.

Freight Revenue per Ton-Mile

Figure 5-4 shows the average freight revenue per ton-mile for air, truck, rail, and pipeline compared to the Producer Price Index (PPI). The PPI measures overall changes in the selling prices received by transportation service providers for their services.

Nominal freight revenue per ton-mile increased for all freight modes; however, revenue increases exceeded producer price increases only for

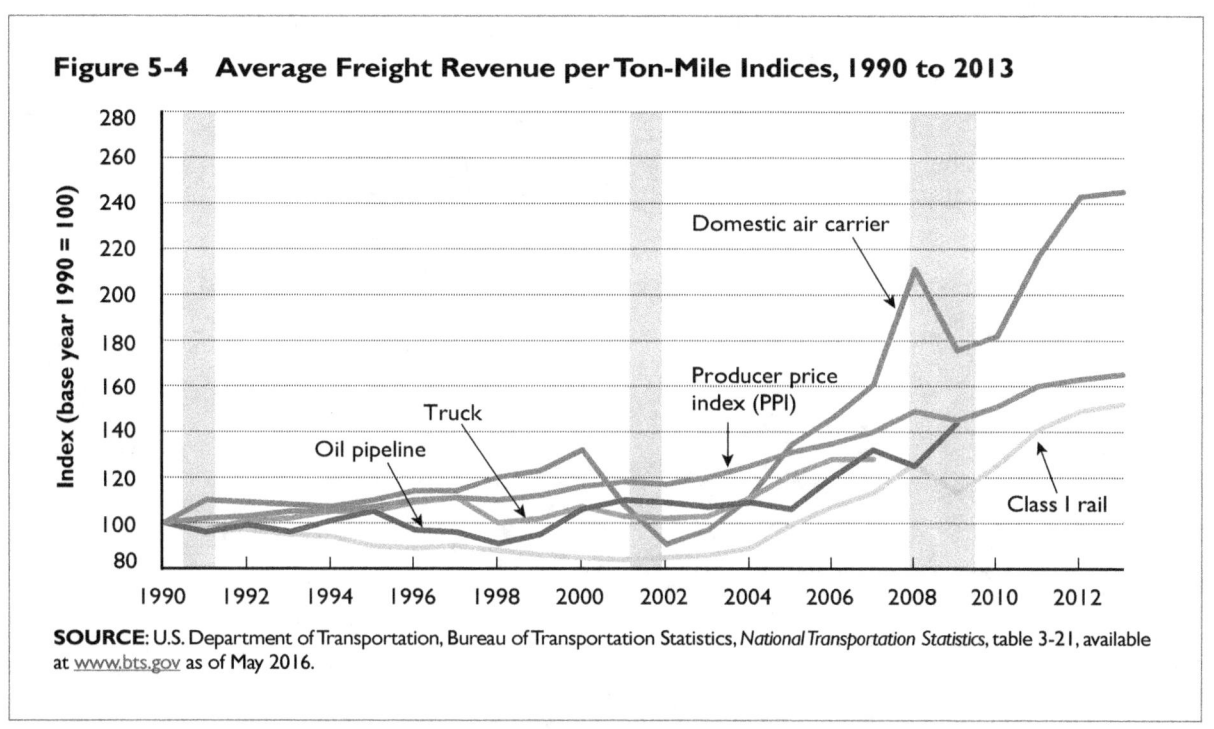

Figure 5-4 Average Freight Revenue per Ton-Mile Indices, 1990 to 2013

SOURCE: U.S. Department of Transportation, Bureau of Transportation Statistics, *National Transportation Statistics*, table 3-21, available at www.bts.gov as of May 2016.

domestic air. Domestic air carriers experienced the largest increase in revenue per ton-mile, increasing 143 percent from 1990 to 2012. Class I railroads, defined as line-haul freight railroads with annual operating revenues of $475.75 million or more as of 2014, experienced a smaller increase in revenue per ton-mile of 48 percent in the same period. Oil pipelines experienced an increase of 44 percent from 1990 to 2009, and trucks experienced the smallest increase of 28 percent from 1990 to 2007. (Data for trucks after 2007 and data for pipelines after 2009 are currently unavailable.)

6 HOUSEHOLD SPENDING ON TRANSPORTATION

Household spending on transportation is one of the largest expenses for American households. It influences many of their personal decisions, including where people live and work. This chapter explores three national measures of household spending on transportation:

1. *Personal Consumption Expenditures*, which measure total national household spending on transportation;

2. The *Consumer Expenditure Survey*, which measures individual household spending on transportation; and

3. *AAA per-mile operating costs* for new vehicles.

Personal Consumption Expenditures

Personal Consumption Expenditures (PCE) is the broadest measure of consumer spending in the American economy. It measures total national household spending on transportation-related goods and services, such as vehicles, fuel, and for-hire transportation. It also measures total national transportation spending by governments, employers, and other organizations on behalf of households—for example, employee transit subsidies. The Bureau of Economic Analysis (BEA) produces PCE using data from a range of sources, including trade organizations, the Census Bureau, the Bureau of Labor Statistics, and the Centers for Medicare & Medicaid Services. PCE measures national aggregate spending only; it does not measure differences in spending among individual households.

In 2014 transportation expenditures accounted for $1.23 trillion (10.4 percent) of PCE, making it the fourth largest category after healthcare, housing, and food (figure 6-1). Transportation

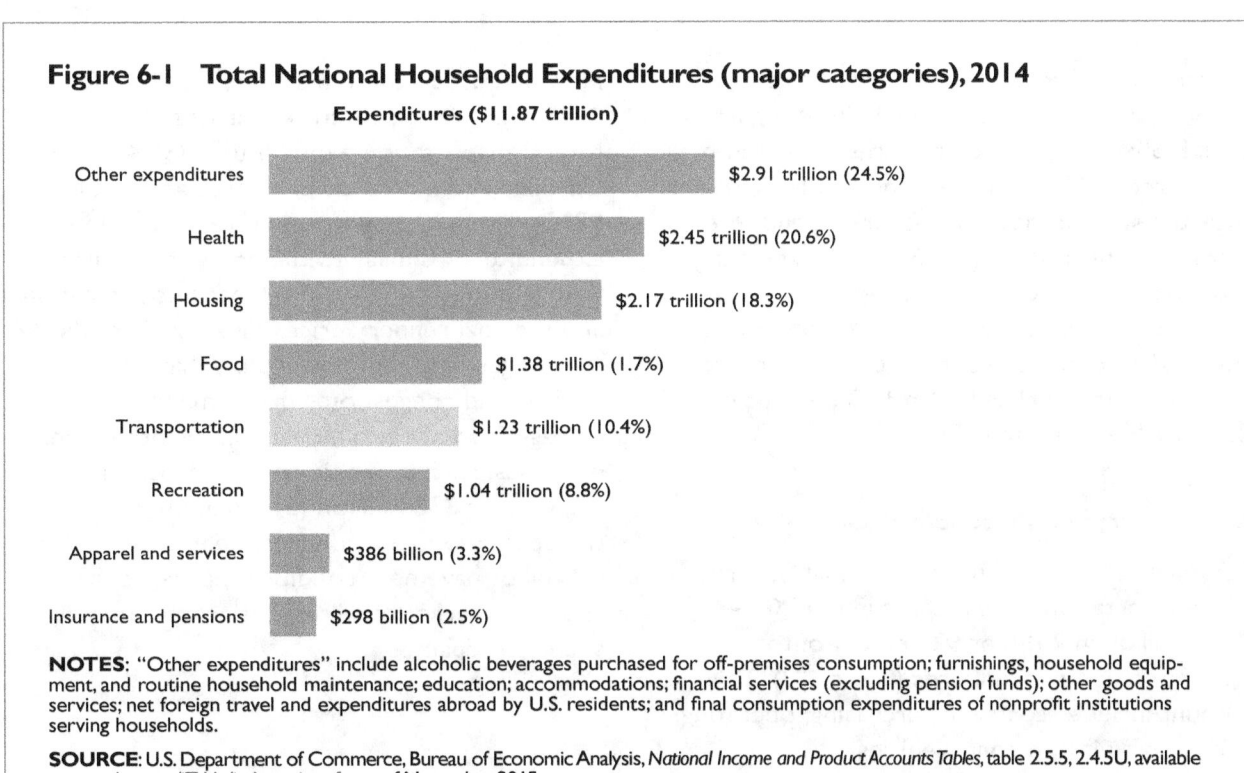

Figure 6-1   Total National Household Expenditures (major categories), 2014

Expenditures ($11.87 trillion)

Other expenditures	$2.91 trillion (24.5%)
Health	$2.45 trillion (20.6%)
Housing	$2.17 trillion (18.3%)
Food	$1.38 trillion (1.7%)
Transportation	$1.23 trillion (10.4%)
Recreation	$1.04 trillion (8.8%)
Apparel and services	$386 billion (3.3%)
Insurance and pensions	$298 billion (2.5%)

NOTES: "Other expenditures" include alcoholic beverages purchased for off-premises consumption; furnishings, household equipment, and routine household maintenance; education; accommodations; financial services (excluding pension funds); other goods and services; net foreign travel and expenditures abroad by U.S. residents; and final consumption expenditures of nonprofit institutions serving households.

SOURCE: U.S. Department of Commerce, Bureau of Economic Analysis, *National Income and Product Accounts Tables*, table 2.5.5, 2.4.5U, available at www.bea.gov/iTable/index_nipa.cfm as of November 2015.

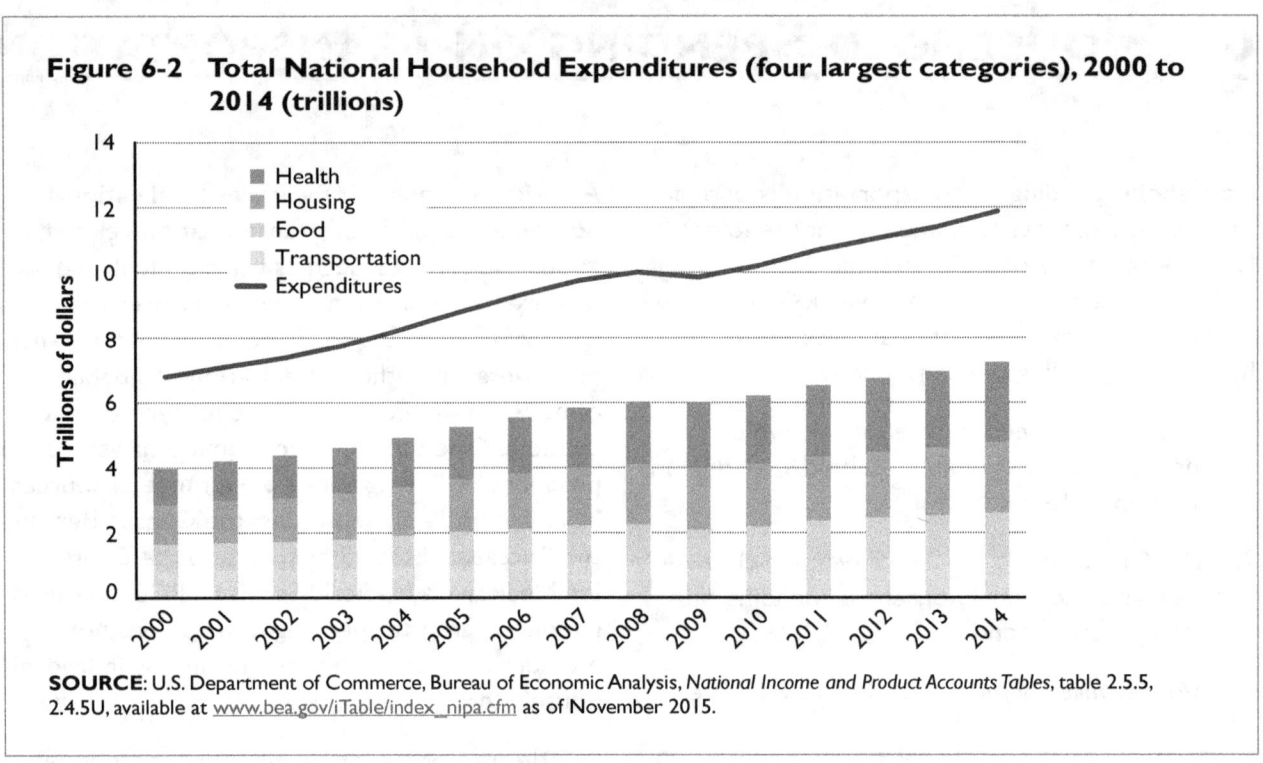

Figure 6-2 Total National Household Expenditures (four largest categories), 2000 to 2014 (trillions)

Legend:
- Health
- Housing
- Food
- Transportation
- Expenditures

Y-axis: Trillions of dollars (0 to 14)
X-axis: 2000 to 2014

SOURCE: U.S. Department of Commerce, Bureau of Economic Analysis, *National Income and Product Accounts Tables*, table 2.5.5, 2.4.5U, available at www.bea.gov/iTable/index_nipa.cfm as of November 2015.

expenditures increased 46.8 percent, from $838 billion in 2000 to $1.23 trillion in 2014 (figure 6-2). However, total expenditures increased by 74.7 percent, from $6.79 trillion to $11.87 trillion over the same period. Moreover, expenditure growth for healthcare (120.5 percent), housing (78.7 percent), and food (71.3 percent) outpaced expenditure growth for transportation. As a result, the percentage of total expenditures for transportation declined from 12.3 percent in 2000 to 10.4 percent in 2014.

Expenditures on Personal Vehicles

Personal vehicles account for the vast majority of transportation expenditures in the PCE—$1.13 trillion in 2014, or 92 percent of total transportation expenditures (figure 6-3). This amount includes costs for purchasing, operating, and maintaining personal vehicles.

New and used vehicle purchases account for $375 billion in expenditures, or one-third of total transportation expenditures (30.4 percent). Gasoline and motor oil purchases account for $373 billion (30.3 percent) in transportation expenditures, similar to the percent expended on vehicle purchases. World oil markets and national and regional refinery prices directly affect the cost of gasoline and motor oil. Vehicle gas mileage and congestion, which limits achievable mileage, also affect the cost. Finally, other vehicle expenses, such as repair costs and insurance, account for $384 billion (31.2 percent) in transportation expenditures. Vehicle age, vehicle reliability, pavement conditions, prices of parts, and local market conditions affect the amount spent on repair.

Expenditures on Intercity and Local For-Hire Transportation

Air passenger travel spending accounted for $52 billion (4.2 percent) of transportation expenditures; intercity bus, train, and ship fares accounted for $6 billion (0.5 percent). Local for-hire transportation services account for $42 billion (3.4 percent) of transportation expenditures. Further disaggregating local transportation shows that mass transit represents 49 percent of expenditures on local for-hire transportation ($21 billion), taxis represent 14 percent ($6 billion), and other services, such as sightseeing buses, account for the remaining 37 percent ($16 billion).

Household Transportation Expenditures

The *Consumer Expenditure Survey* (CE), administered by the Bureau of Labor Statistics (BLS), measures individual household spending in the United States. A nationally representative sample of households provides detailed information on expenditures, income, and household characteristics. The CE is the only Federal survey that contains information on the complete range of expenditures for individual households, including transportation.

The CE shows that households in the United States spent an average of $9,073 on transportation in 2014, making transportation the second largest household expenditure category (representing 18.0 percent of total expenditures) after housing (figure 6-4). Transportation accounts for a greater percentage of the CE than the PCE because the CE includes only direct household expenditures, whereas the PCE includes expenditures on behalf of households (box 6-1).

Figure 6-3   Total National Household Transportation Expenditures 2014

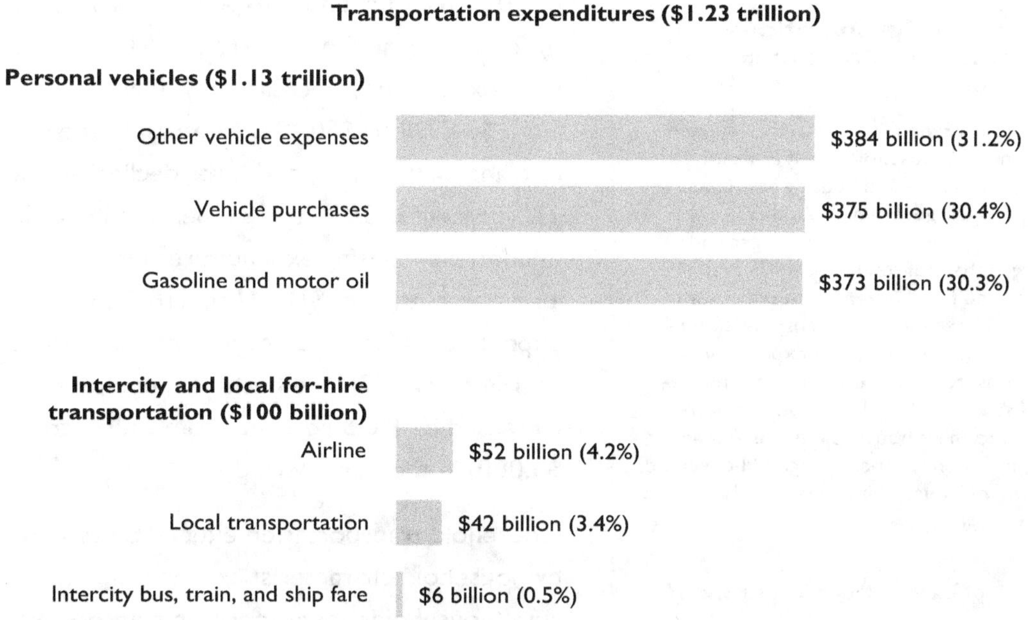

Transportation expenditures ($1.23 trillion)

Personal vehicles ($1.13 trillion)

Other vehicle expenses	$384 billion (31.2%)
Vehicle purchases	$375 billion (30.4%)
Gasoline and motor oil	$373 billion (30.3%)

Intercity and local for-hire transportation ($100 billion)

Airline	$52 billion (4.2%)
Local transportation	$42 billion (3.4%)
Intercity bus, train, and ship fare	$6 billion (0.5%)

NOTE: "Other vehicle expenses" include vehicle insurance, vehicle parts, and maintenance and repair costs.

SOURCE: U.S. Department of Commerce, Bureau of Economic Analysis, *National Income and Product Accounts Tables*, table 2.5.5, 2.4.5U, available at www.bea.gov/iTable/index_nipa.cfm as of November 2015.

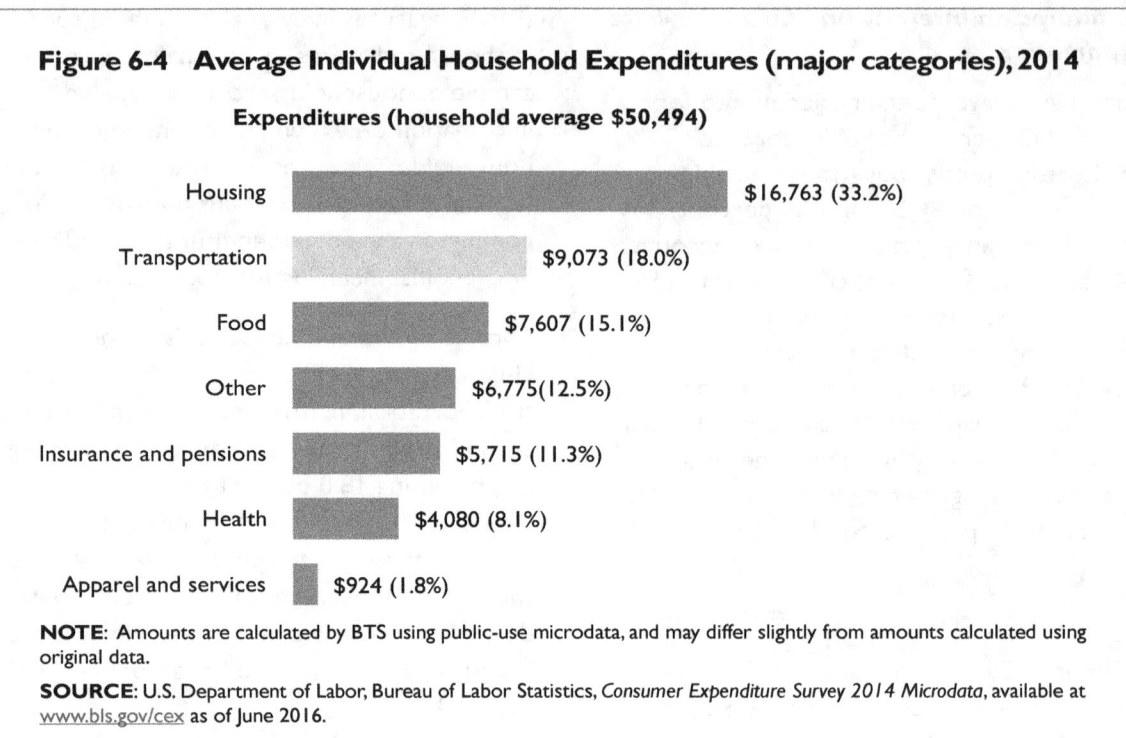

Figure 6-4   Average Individual Household Expenditures (major categories), 2014

Expenditures (household average $50,494)

Housing	$16,763 (33.2%)
Transportation	$9,073 (18.0%)
Food	$7,607 (15.1%)
Other	$6,775(12.5%)
Insurance and pensions	$5,715 (11.3%)
Health	$4,080 (8.1%)
Apparel and services	$924 (1.8%)

NOTE: Amounts are calculated by BTS using public-use microdata, and may differ slightly from amounts calculated using original data.

SOURCE: U.S. Department of Labor, Bureau of Labor Statistics, *Consumer Expenditure Survey 2014 Microdata*, available at www.bls.gov/cex as of June 2016.

Box 6-1   Personal Consumption Expenditures and the Consumer Expenditure Survey

Personal Consumption Expenditures includes expenditures made on behalf of households such as healthcare premiums paid by businesses and housing assistance from non-profits and the government. As a result, healthcare and housing expenditures are larger and account for a larger share of total expenditures than in the Consumer Expenditure Survey, which only examines direct household expenditures. Transportation as a percentage of personal consumption expenditures is the most useful measure for discussions about household needs because it includes all of the expenditures that society makes to meet household needs. At the same time, transportation as a percentage of household expenditures is the most useful measure for discussions about household budgets.

SOURCE: Bureau of Transportation Statistics, 2016

Average annual household transportation expenditures have increased more slowly than other major expenditures (figure 6-5). From 2000 to 2014, transportation expenditures increased by 22.3 percent, from $7,417 to $9,073, while total expenditures increased by 44.9 percent, from $34,839 to $50,494. As a result, the share of transportation expenditures declined from 21.3 percent in 2000 to 18.0 percent in 2014. In contrast, housing expenditures increased by 45.8 percent (from $11,494 to $16,763), food expenditures increased by 47.3 percent (from $5,164 to $7,607), and health expenditures increased by 110.5 percent (from $1,938 to $4,080) in the same period.

Household transportation expenditures vary by household characteristics. For example, rural households spent more on transportation ($9,102) than urban households ($8,772) in 2014, in part because rural households have higher rates of vehicle ownership and drive more miles

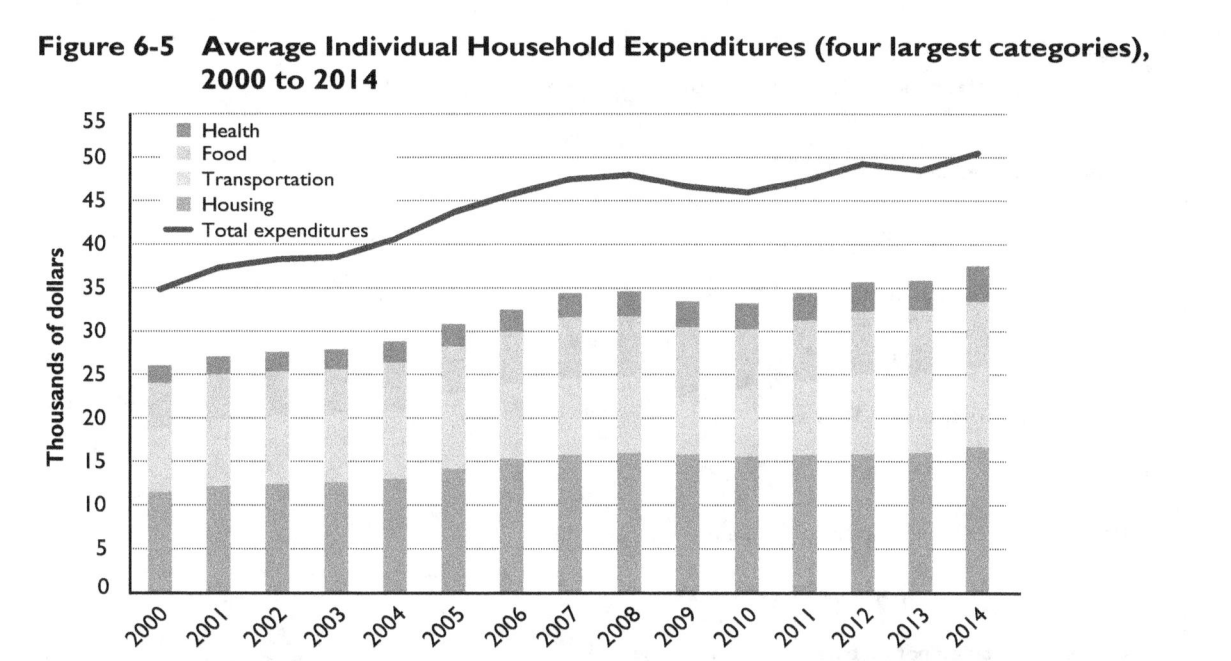

Figure 6-5 Average Individual Household Expenditures (four largest categories), 2000 to 2014

NOTE: Amounts are calculated by BTS using public-use microdata, and may differ slightly from amounts calculated using original data.

SOURCE: U.S. Department of Labor, Bureau of Labor Statistics, *Consumer Expenditure Survey 2014 Microdata*, available at www.bls.gov/cex as of June 2016.

per capita.[1] In addition, households without vehicles spend lower amounts on transportation.

Average annual expenditures are a useful measure of household spending on transportation; at the same time, however, spending for an individual household can vary greatly from year to year. For example, households have much higher expenditures in years that they purchase vehicles. Year-to-year changes in gasoline prices and vehicle insurance premiums can also affect expenditures for an individual household. The CE does not capture these changes for households because it is a cross-sectional survey and samples a different group of households each year.

Expenditures on Personal Vehicles

The average household devotes the vast majority of its transportation budget (93.6 percent of $9,073 or $8,492) to purchasing, operating, and maintaining private vehicles (figure 6-6). Vehicle purchases account for 36.4 percent ($3,301) of transportation expenditures, gasoline and motor oil account for 27.2 percent ($2,468), and other vehicle expenses, such as repairs and insurance account for 30.0 percent ($2,723).

Expenditures on Intercity and Local For-Hire Transportation

Public transportation accounts for the remaining 7 percent ($581) of household transportation expenditures. Within public transportation expenditures, intercity travel represents 82 percent ($474) of expenditures—64 percent ($370) for airline fares; 14 percent ($84) for

---

[1] For more information on travel behavior and demographics, please see U.S. Department of Transportation Federal Highway Administration, *Summary of Travel Trends: 2009 National Household Travel Survey*, available at http://nhts.ornl.gov/2009/pub/stt.pdf.

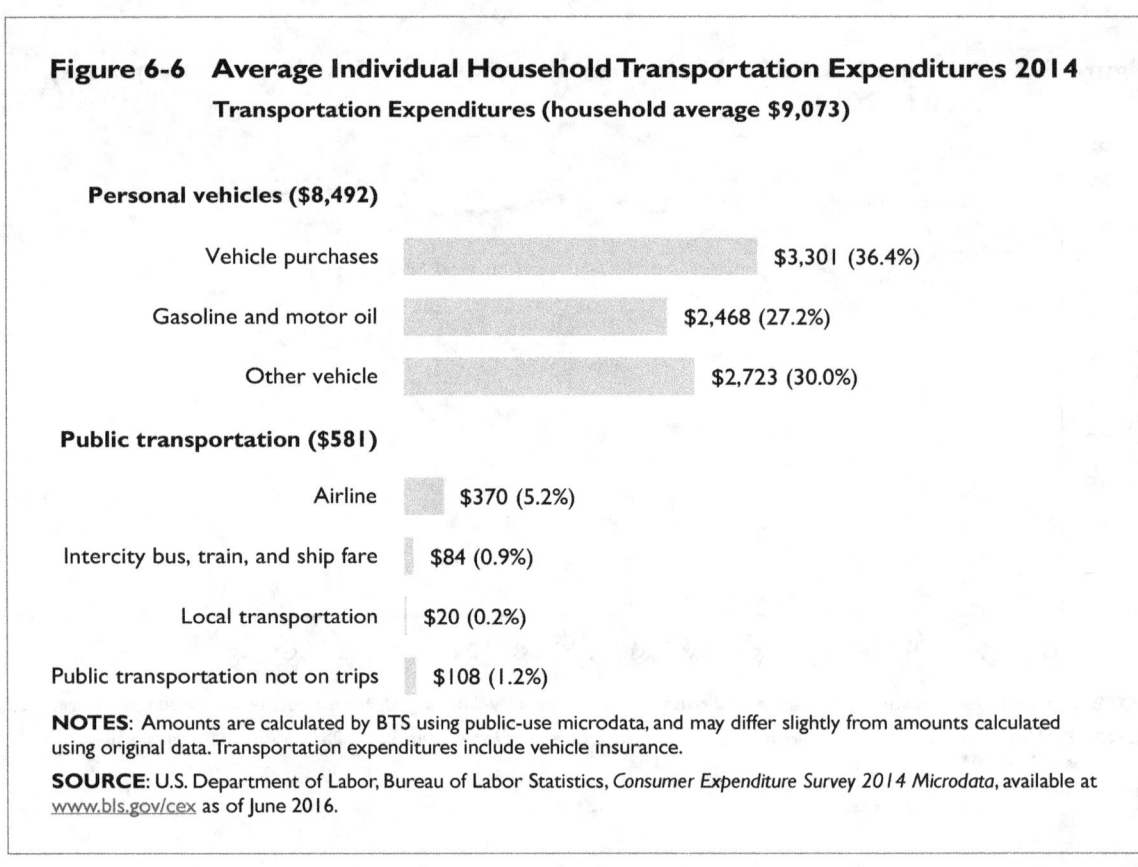

Figure 6-6   Average Individual Household Transportation Expenditures 2014

Transportation Expenditures (household average $9,073)

Personal vehicles ($8,492)

Vehicle purchases — $3,301 (36.4%)

Gasoline and motor oil — $2,468 (27.2%)

Other vehicle — $2,723 (30.0%)

Public transportation ($581)

Airline — $370 (5.2%)

Intercity bus, train, and ship fare — $84 (0.9%)

Local transportation — $20 (0.2%)

Public transportation not on trips — $108 (1.2%)

NOTES: Amounts are calculated by BTS using public-use microdata, and may differ slightly from amounts calculated using original data. Transportation expenditures include vehicle insurance.

SOURCE: U.S. Department of Labor, Bureau of Labor Statistics, *Consumer Expenditure Survey 2014 Microdata*, available at www.bls.gov/cex as of June 2016.

bus, train, and ship fares; and 3 percent ($20) for local transportation in other cities. Local public transportation accounts for the remaining 19 percent ($108) of public transportation expenditures.

Transportation Expenditures and Income

Households spend relatively similar percentages on transportation across all income categories (table 6-1), with the percentage ranging from 15 to 19 percent. While the percentages remain relatively similar, households in the top income quintile spent nearly five times as much per year as households in the bottom income quintile—$16,788 versus $3,555.

Higher income households spend more on transportation because they are more likely to own vehicles: 97 percent of households on the top income quintile have at least one vehicle, compared with 63 percent in the bottom income quintile. Moreover, higher income households have greater numbers of vehicles. Households in the top income quintile own an average of 2.8 vehicles per household, whereas households in the bottom income quintile own 0.9 vehicles per household.

Per-Mile Vehicle Operating Costs

The American Automobile Association (AAA) collects data on automobile operating costs annually and publishes per-mile cost estimates for new vehicles driven 15,000 miles a year for 5 years (box 6-2). Figure 6-7 shows vehicle operating costs from 2004 to 2014. In 2014 dollars, operating costs declined 15 percent from

Table 6-1 Average Individual Household Expenditures by Income Quintile, 2014

Annual income by quintile	Annual spending	Vehicles per household	Households with at least one vehicle	Transportation spending per household	Percentage of annual spending
All quintiles	$53,495	1.9	87%	$9,073	17%
First quintile ($18,362 and below)	$23,713	0.9	63%	$3,555	15%
Second quintile ($18,363–$35,681)	$33,546	1.4	86%	$5,696	17%
Third quintile ($35,682–$59,549)	$45,395	1.9	93%	$8,475	19%
Fourth quintile ($59,550–$99,620)	$60,417	2.3	96%	$10,844	18%
Fifth quintile ($99,621 and above)	$104,363	2.8	97%	$16,788	16%

SOURCE: U.S. Department of Labor, Bureau of Labor Statistics, *Consumer Expenditure Survey*, available at www.bls.gov/cex as of June 2016.

Box 6-2 Per-Mile Vehicle Operating Expenses

The American Automobile Association (AAA) publishes per-mile vehicle operating cost estimates in *Your Driving Costs*. To calculate the costs, AAA estimates annual costs for small, medium, and large sedans using data from five top-selling current-year vehicles for each group. AAA's estimates assume that drivers drive 15,000 miles a year and trade in vehicles after 5 years. Fixed costs include depreciation, insurance, licensing, registration, taxes, and finance charges.

SOURCE: Bureau of Transportation Statistics, 2016

$0.68 per mile in 2004 to $0.58 per mile in 2014. The primary reason is that fixed ownership costs, which represent 70 percent of operating costs ($0.41 per mile in 2014) for new vehicles, declined by 23 percent in the same period. Fixed ownership costs include depreciation, vehicle insurance, license and registration fees, and finance charges. Gasoline, a highly salient cost to consumers because they see prices posted at every gas station, represents 19 percent ($0.11 per mile in 2014) of operating costs. Finally, maintenance and tires account for the remaining 11 percent ($0.06 per mile in 2014) of operating costs.

Figure 6-7 Per-Mile Costs of Owning and Operating an Automobile, 2004 to 2014 (2014 dollars)

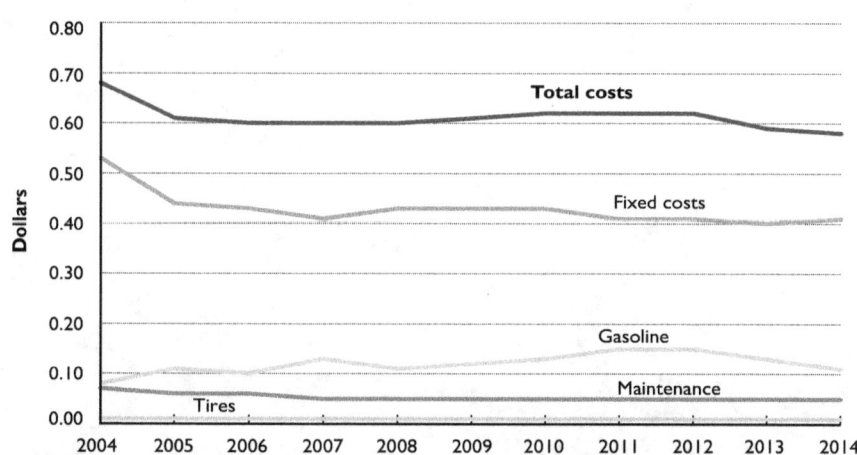

NOTE: Fixed costs include depreciation, insurance, licensing, registration, taxes, and finance charges.

SOURCE: American Automobile Association, *Your Driving Costs*, as cited in U.S. Department of Transportation, Bureau of Transportation Statistics, *National Transportation Statistics*, Table 3-17, available at www.bts.gov as of June 2016.

7 GOVERNMENT REVENUES AND EXPENDITURES

Introduction

Federal, state, and local governments play a major role in providing transportation services and infrastructure in the United States. Governments spend funds on critical activities like building highways, operating the Nation's air traffic control system, and maintaining transit facilities. These funds come from several government revenue sources, including user fees, taxes, bonds, and grants.

This chapter presents data on government transportation revenue and spending from three sources:

1. Government Transportation Financial Statistics (box 7-1), which examines transportation revenue and spending at the federal level and at the state and local level;

2. *State Transportation Statistics* (STS) and the Survey of State Funding for Public Transportation from the American Association of State Highway and Transportation Officials (AASHTO), which examine transportation revenue and spending in individual states; and

Box 7-1   Government Transportation Financial Statistics

Government Transportation Financial Statistics, a publication of the Bureau of Transportation Statistics, provides information on transportation-related revenue and expenditures for all levels of government and for all modes of transportation. It aggregates data from a variety of sources, including the Office of Management and Budget's Public Budget Database, the Federal Highway Administration's *Highway Statistics Report*, the National Transit Database, the FAA's *Airport Financial Report*, tax data from the Bureau of Economic Analysis, and the U.S. Census Bureau's *Survey of State and Local Government Finances*.

3. National Highway Construction Cost Index (NHCCI), which measures the prices that state transportation departments pay for roadway construction materials and services.

Government Transportation Revenue

Government transportation revenue comes from user taxes and fees, such as gasoline taxes and tolls, air ticket taxes, and general revenues, as well as income from investing transportation funds and receipts from fines and penalties. In 2012, revenue collected and dedicated to transportation programs totaled $350.4 billion. A portion of this revenue ($180.2 billion, or 51.4 percent) comes from taxes and charges levied on transportation-related activities, while $170.3 billion (48.6 percent) comes from non-transportation-related activities but supports transportation programs (e.g., state or local sales or property taxes used to finance transportation projects). On top of the $350.4 billion, governments collected an additional $21.4 billion in revenue from transportation-related activities but diverted this revenue to non-transportation programs (e.g., revenue from motor fuel taxes directed to the general fund for other uses). In real 2009 dollars, total revenue collected and dedicated to transportation programs increased by 43.3 percent from 1995 to 2012 (figure 7-1).

Sources of Government Transportation Revenue

Highway and aviation, which have trust funds supported by dedicated taxes, accounted for 95.6 percent of federal transportation revenue in 2012 (figure 7-2). The Federal Government collected $40.3 billion (72.6 percent) in highway revenues and $12.8 billion (23.1 percent) in aviation revenues, as well as $2.3 billion (4.1 percent) in

Box 7-2 Government Transportation Revenue

Transportation revenue includes taxes, charges, and fees collected by governments from transportation and non-transportation activities and allocated to transportation programs. Income from investing transportation funds and receipts from fines and penalties are also treated as transportation revenue. For reporting, transportation revenue is classified and grouped into two categories: *own-source revenue* and *supporting revenue*, minus *transportation revenue directed to other uses*.

Own-source revenue refers to taxes and charges levied on transportation-related activities and used specifically for transportation. Most of these revenue sources are user fees charged to users of the transportation system. Examples include:

- Excise taxes such as motor fuel taxes and aviation taxes

- Property taxes such as motor vehicle taxes

- Income taxes such as corporate taxes paid by transportation companies

- Charges such as tolls and motor vehicle license fees

- Fines and penalties such as speeding and parking violation tickets

- Investment income such as interest income from Highway Trust Fund balance

- Income from concession agreements where a publicly owned transportation infrastructure is operated on a concession basis by a private company

Supporting revenue includes funds that are collected from non-transportation-related activities but dedicated to support transportation programs. Examples include receipts received by state and local governments from sales or property taxes to finance transportation projects.

Revenue directed to other uses includes funds that are raised from transportation-related activities but used to finance programs other than transportation. An example is receipts generated from motor fuel taxes that are directed to the general fund for other uses.

SOURCE: U.S. Department of Transportation, Bureau of Transportation Statistics, 2016.

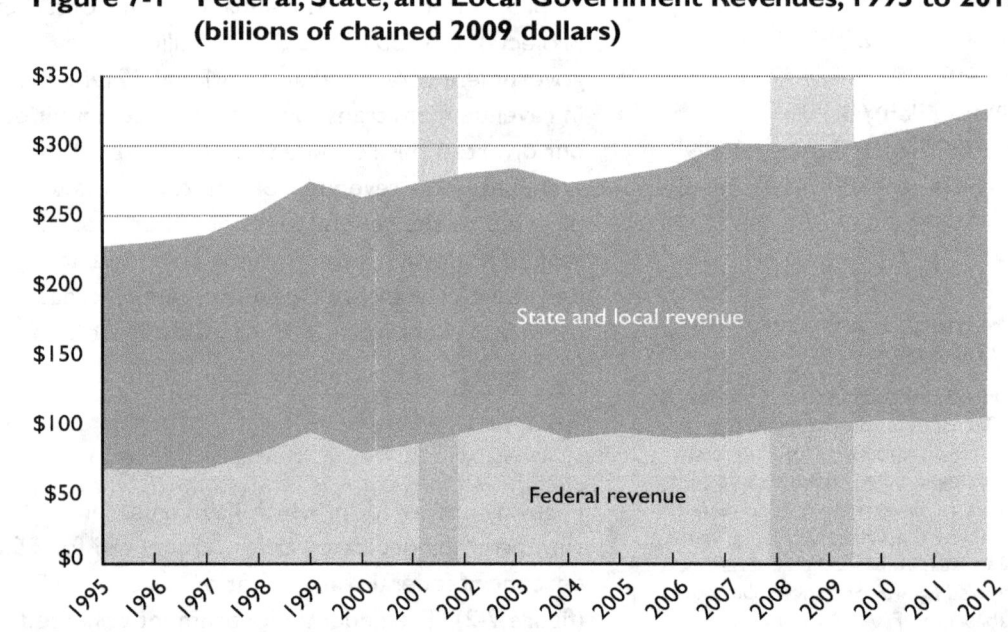

Figure 7-1   Federal, State, and Local Government Revenues, 1995 to 2012 (billions of chained 2009 dollars)

NOTE: Revenue includes own-source revenue and supporting revenue, but does not include revenue diverted to other uses.

SOURCE: U.S. Department of Transportation, Bureau of Transportation Statistics, *Government Transportation Financial Statistics 2014*, Table 9-B, available at www.bts.gov as of July 2016.

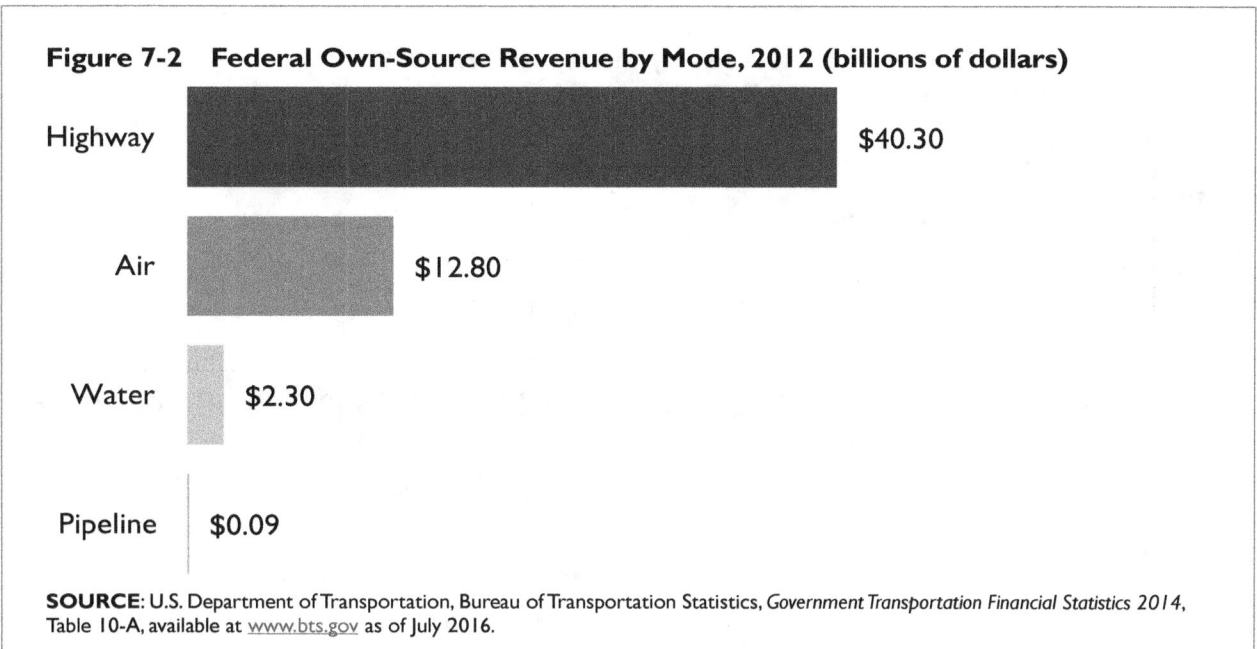

Figure 7-2 Federal Own-Source Revenue by Mode, 2012 (billions of dollars)

Highway $40.30

Air $12.80

Water $2.30

Pipeline $0.09

SOURCE: U.S. Department of Transportation, Bureau of Transportation Statistics, *Government Transportation Financial Statistics 2014*, Table 10-A, available at www.bts.gov as of July 2016.

water transportation revenues and $90.0 million (0.2 percent) in pipeline revenues.

In real 2009 dollars, highway trust fund revenues decreased by 8.7 percent from 1995 to 2012 (figure 7-3). The Federal Government has not increased the federal taxes for gasoline and diesel—18.4 cents per gallon for gasoline and 24.4 cents per gallon—since October 1997, causing real revenues to decline. Revenues also declined because vehicle gas mileage improved over the last two decades and because vehicle miles traveled declined during the 2007 to 2009 recession. Highway revenue data also show a spike in 1999 because legislative changes shifted some fuel tax revenues from fiscal year 1998 to fiscal year 1999.[1] Highway revenues slowly increased since the recession, as did air revenues, but remain below historic levels.

State and local governments collected $237.6 billion of the $350.4 billion (67.8 percent) in government revenues. Of this revenue, the state

and local governments collected $124.7 billion from transportation-related activities, most of which is from highway revenue sources ($84.8 billion, or 68.0 percent of transportation revenue in 2012), which include fuel taxes, motor vehicle taxes, and tolls (figure 7-4). Aviation-related revenue ($18.3 billion, 14.7 percent) comes from landing fees, terminal area rentals, and several other sources. Transit revenue ($17.6 billion, 14.1 percent) is almost entirely from fares. In real 2009 dollars, highway, aviation, and water revenues all declined during the recession, although highway revenue has since exceeded pre-recession levels (figure 7-5).

Revenue collected from transportation-related activity and dedicated to transportation programs continues to fall short of government transportation expenditures. In 2012 transportation revenues covered 56.3 percent of expenditures. The gap between transportation revenues and expenditures has declined since 2009 when revenues covered 51.0 percent of expenditures. When revenues do not cover expenditures, general tax receipts (e.g., from sales and property taxes), trust fund balances, and borrowing are needed to cover shortages.

[1] The Tax Payer Relief Act of 1997 allowed taxpayers to delay paying fuel taxes due in August and September 1998 until Oct. 5, 1998. The act shifted about $6 billion in Highway Trust Fund receipts from fiscal year 1998 to fiscal year 1999 as a result.

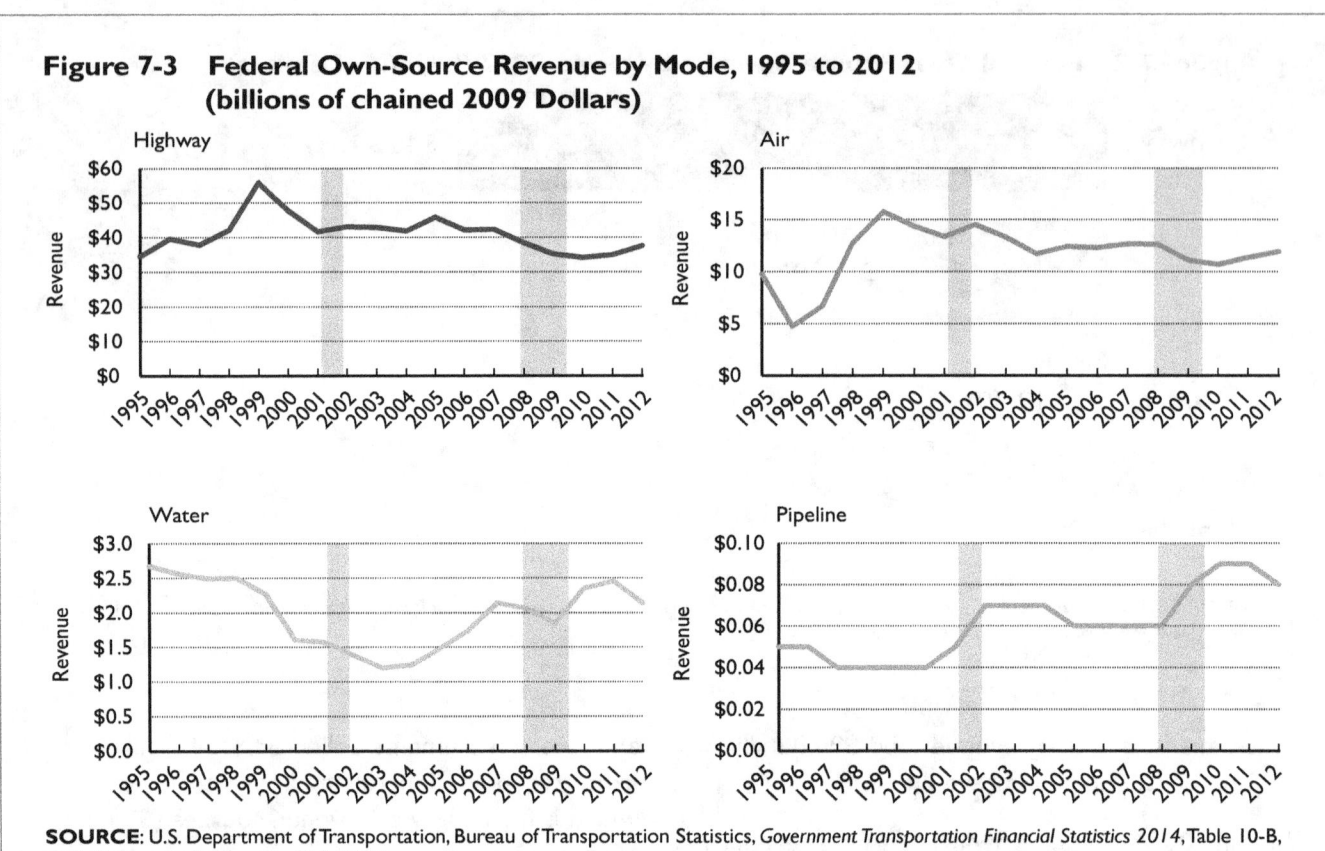

Figure 7-3   Federal Own-Source Revenue by Mode, 1995 to 2012
(billions of chained 2009 Dollars)

SOURCE: U.S. Department of Transportation, Bureau of Transportation Statistics, *Government Transportation Financial Statistics 2014*, Table 10-B, available at www.bts.gov as of July 2016.

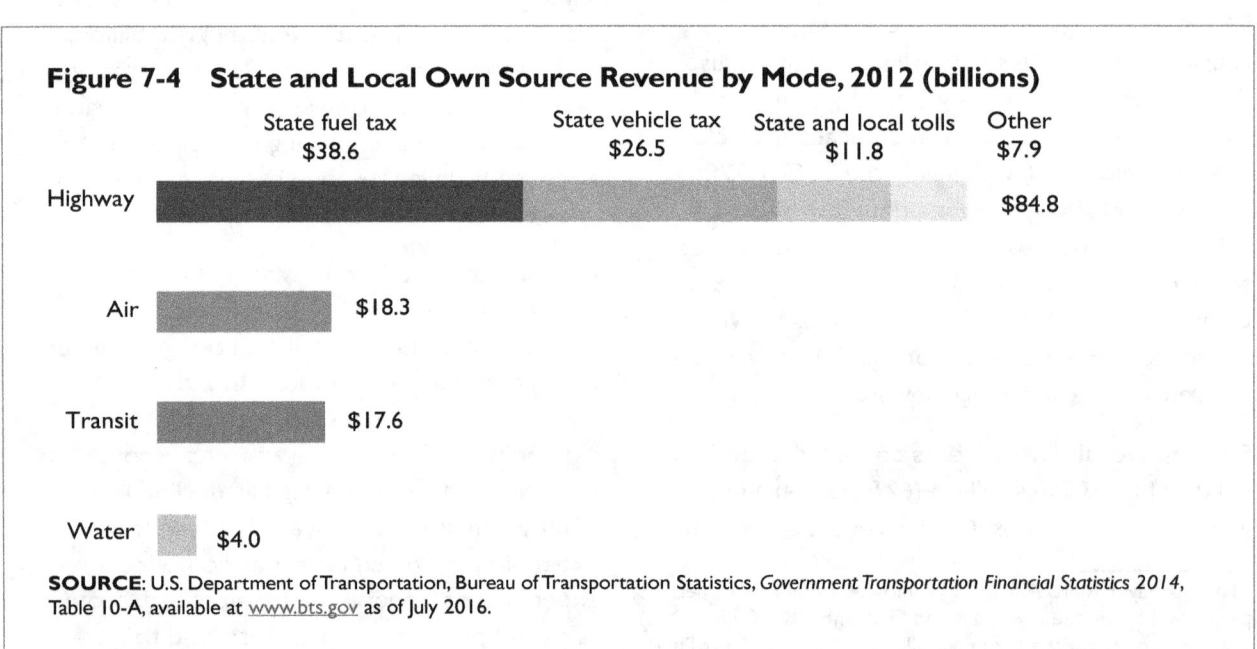

Figure 7-4   State and Local Own Source Revenue by Mode, 2012 (billions)

SOURCE: U.S. Department of Transportation, Bureau of Transportation Statistics, *Government Transportation Financial Statistics 2014*, Table 10-A, available at www.bts.gov as of July 2016.

Figure 7-5 State and Local Own Source Revenue by Mode, 1995 to 2012 (billions of chained 2009 dollars)

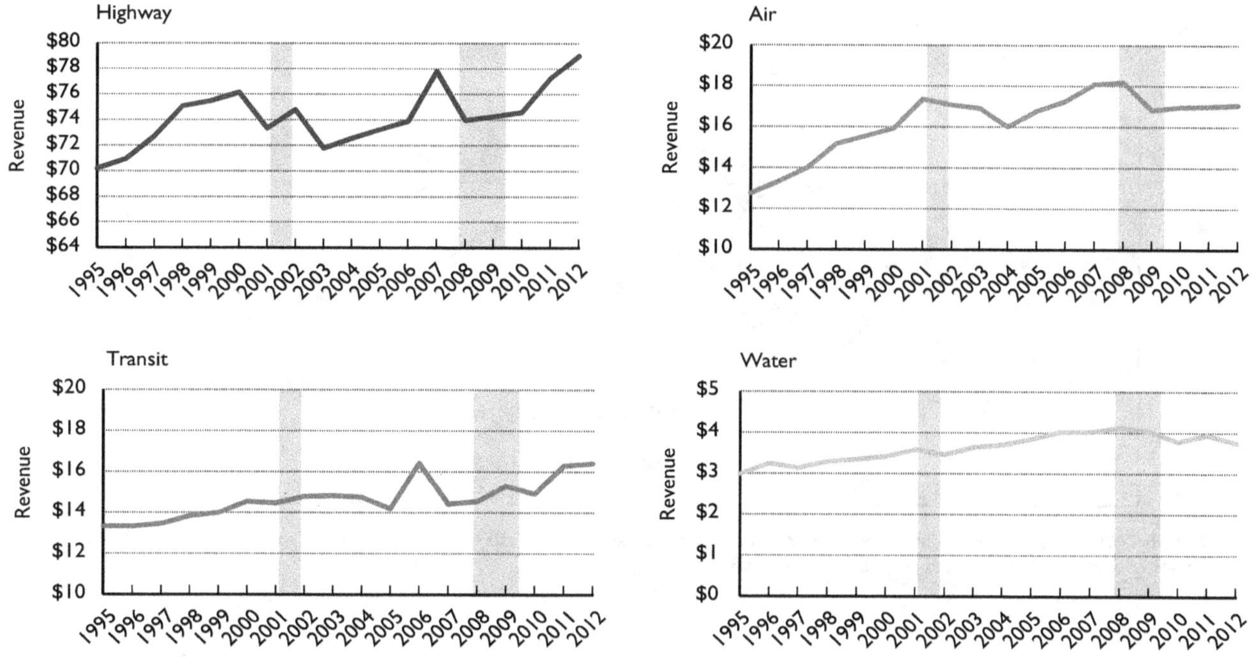

SOURCE: U.S. Department of Transportation, Bureau of Transportation Statistics, *Government Transportation Financial Statistics 2014*, Table 10-B, available at www.bts.gov as of July 2016.

Box 7-3 Government Transportation Expenditures

Transportation expenditures are outlays the government pays to provide an efficient and safe transportation system, regardless of the sources of funding and which agencies make the payments. Expenditures include both capital investments and money spent to maintain and operate the transportation system. Government expenditures on transportation that do not support the transportation system, such as paying for military shipments, are not included.

Federal expenditures are collected from sources, which include the *Office of Management and Budget: Analytical Perspective* and the Federal Highway Administration's *Highway Statistics*. State and local expenditure data comes primarily from the U.S. Census Bureau's *State and Local Government Finances* and from the National Transit Database. State and local expenditure financed by federal funding is shown separately. This makes it possible to see federal expenditures including funding provided to state and local governments, and state and local expenditures including federal funds received, and avoids double-counting those federal funds. It is possible to look at expenditure trends by level of government based on what level of government is generating the funds, or at which level the funds are spent.

SOURCE: U.S. Department of Transportation, Bureau of Transportation Statistics, 2016.

Government Transportation Spending

Most government spending on transportation takes place at the state and local levels, although state and local capital expenditures are often paid for in part with federal funds (box 7-3). In 2012, the Federal Government spent $38.5 billion on transportation (excluding federal transfers to states), and state and local governments spent $281.4 billion (including expenditures paid for with federal transfers such as the Federal-Aid Highway Program and the Airport and Airway Trust Fund).

In real 2009 dollars, transportation expenditures at all levels of government have increased since

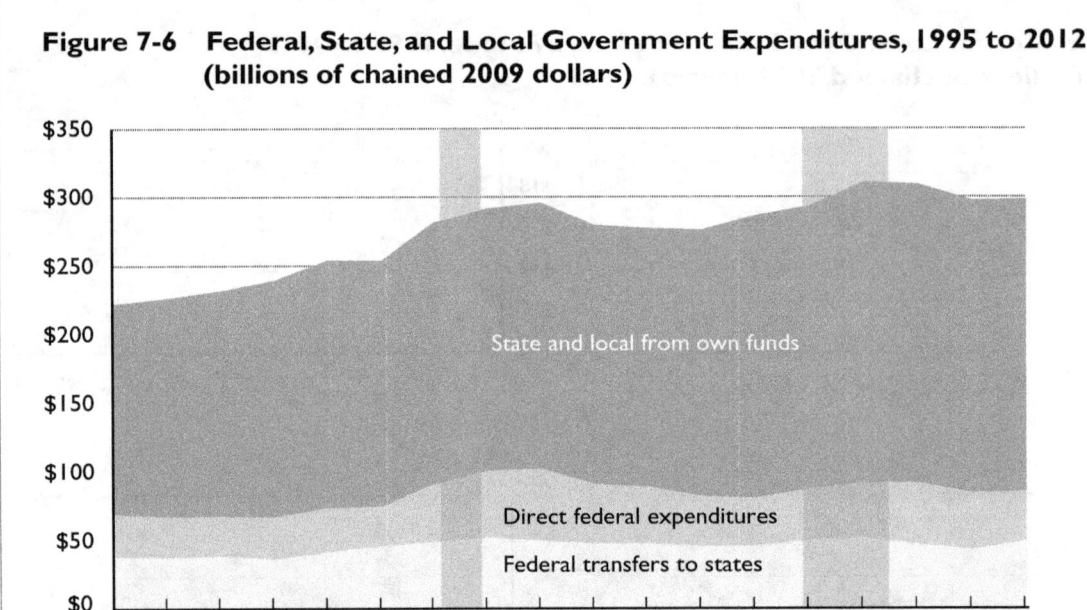

Figure 7-6   Federal, State, and Local Government Expenditures, 1995 to 2012 (billions of chained 2009 dollars)

SOURCE: U.S. Department of Transportation, Bureau of Transportation Statistics, *Government Transportation Financial Statistics 2014*, Tables 18-B and 19-B, available at www.bts.gov as of July 2016.

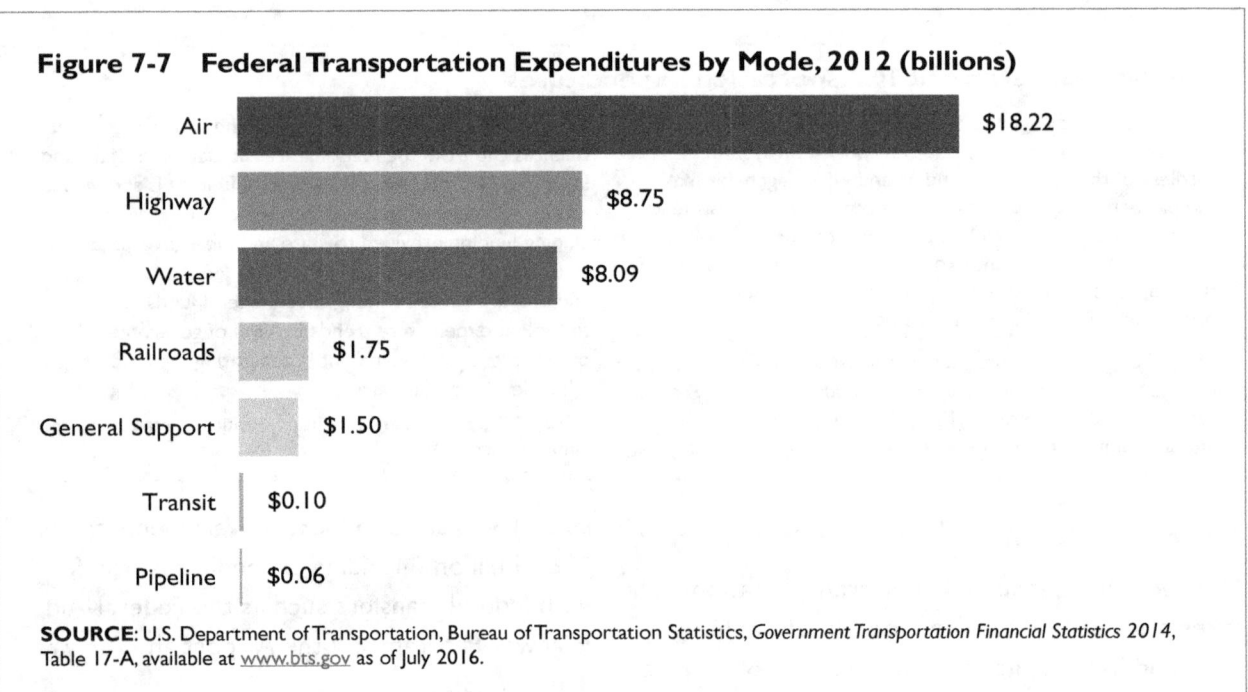

Figure 7-7   Federal Transportation Expenditures by Mode, 2012 (billions)

SOURCE: U.S. Department of Transportation, Bureau of Transportation Statistics, *Government Transportation Financial Statistics 2014*, Table 17-A, available at www.bts.gov as of July 2016.

1995 (figure 7-6). From 1995 to 2012, real state and local expenditures (including expenditures paid for with federal funds) increased by 36.8 percent, while federal expenditures increased by 17.3 percent. Governments increased transportation spending following the 2007 to 2009 recession to stimulate the economy. In 2009 the Federal Government enacted the American Recovery and Reinvestment Act of 2009, which authorized $48.1 billion in transportation stimulus spending. As a result, transportation expenditures for the Federal government reached peaks in 2008 and 2009.

Federal Transportation Spending by Mode

Most federal spending (excluding federal transfers to states) is for aviation ($18.2 billion in 2012, or 47.4 percent) and highways ($8.7 billion, or 22.7 percent) (figure 7-7 and box 7-3). In real 2009 dollars, aviation spending peaked in 2002, when governments increased spending on airport

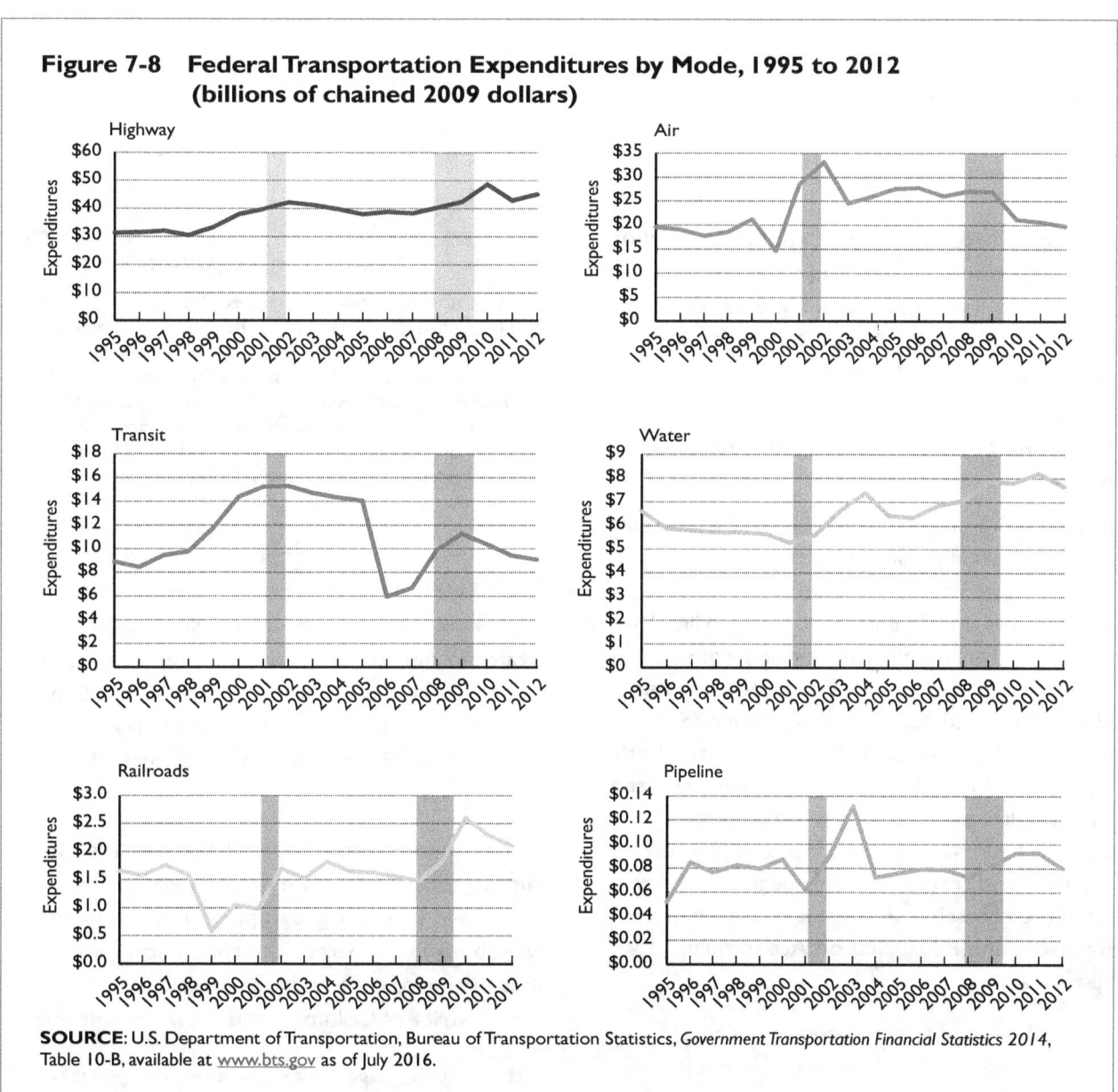

Figure 7-8   Federal Transportation Expenditures by Mode, 1995 to 2012 (billions of chained 2009 dollars)

SOURCE: U.S. Department of Transportation, Bureau of Transportation Statistics, *Government Transportation Financial Statistics 2014*, Table 10-B, available at www.bts.gov as of July 2016.

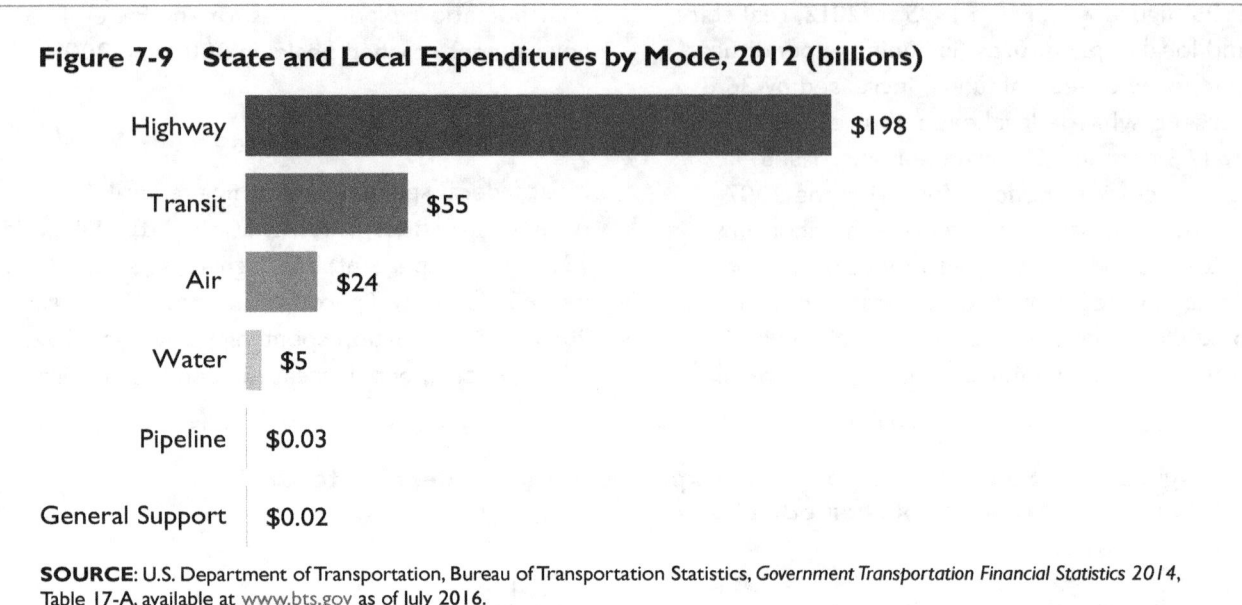

Figure 7-9 State and Local Expenditures by Mode, 2012 (billions)

Mode	Amount
Highway	$198
Transit	$55
Air	$24
Water	$5
Pipeline	$0.03
General Support	$0.02

SOURCE: U.S. Department of Transportation, Bureau of Transportation Statistics, *Government Transportation Financial Statistics 2014*, Table 17-A, available at www.bts.gov as of July 2016.

security in response to the September 11, 2001 terrorist attacks and since has decreased by 42.3 percent (figure 7-8). Federal highway spending peaked in 2010 with the recession stimulus spending, and then declined.

State and Local Transportation Spending by Mode

In 2012, 70.2 percent ($197.5 billion) of state and local spending on transportation (including expenditures paid for with federal grants) went to highways, and 19.6 percent ($55.1 billion) went to transit (figure 7-9). The remaining amount went to air ($23.6 billion, 8.4 percent), water ($5.2 billion, 1.8 percent), and pipeline ($.03 billion, 0.01 percent). In real 2009 dollars, both highway and transit expenditure have increased over the last two decades—highways by 34.0 percent and transit by 36.5 percent (figure 7-10). Highway and transit spending peaked in 2009 after the recession as a result of the American Recovery and Rehabilitation Act stimulus spending.

Figure 7-11 shows the percentage of total expenditures that each state and its local governments spent on transportation in 2013

Box 7-4 State Transportation Finance

State transportation expenditure data come from the U.S. Census Bureau's State and Local Government Finances, which conducts a full census of state and local governments every 5 years and a sample survey in the intervening years. Federal and state spending on transit was collected by a survey of state transportation departments conducted by the American Association of State Highway and Transportation Officials. These data do not include local government expenditures on transit.

(box 7-4).[2] There is a regional pattern with higher expenditures in low-density, resource-rich states in the northern Great Plains. These states have considerable demand for transportation to support industries that rely on bulky, transportation-intensive products such as oil, coal, and minerals.

States and local governments also allocate funds among transportation modes differently because they have different geographies and economies, which lead to different transportation needs. For example, state and local governments in the District of Columbia and New York devote

---

[2] The percentages spent in each state may change due to annual fluctuations in state transportation expenditures.

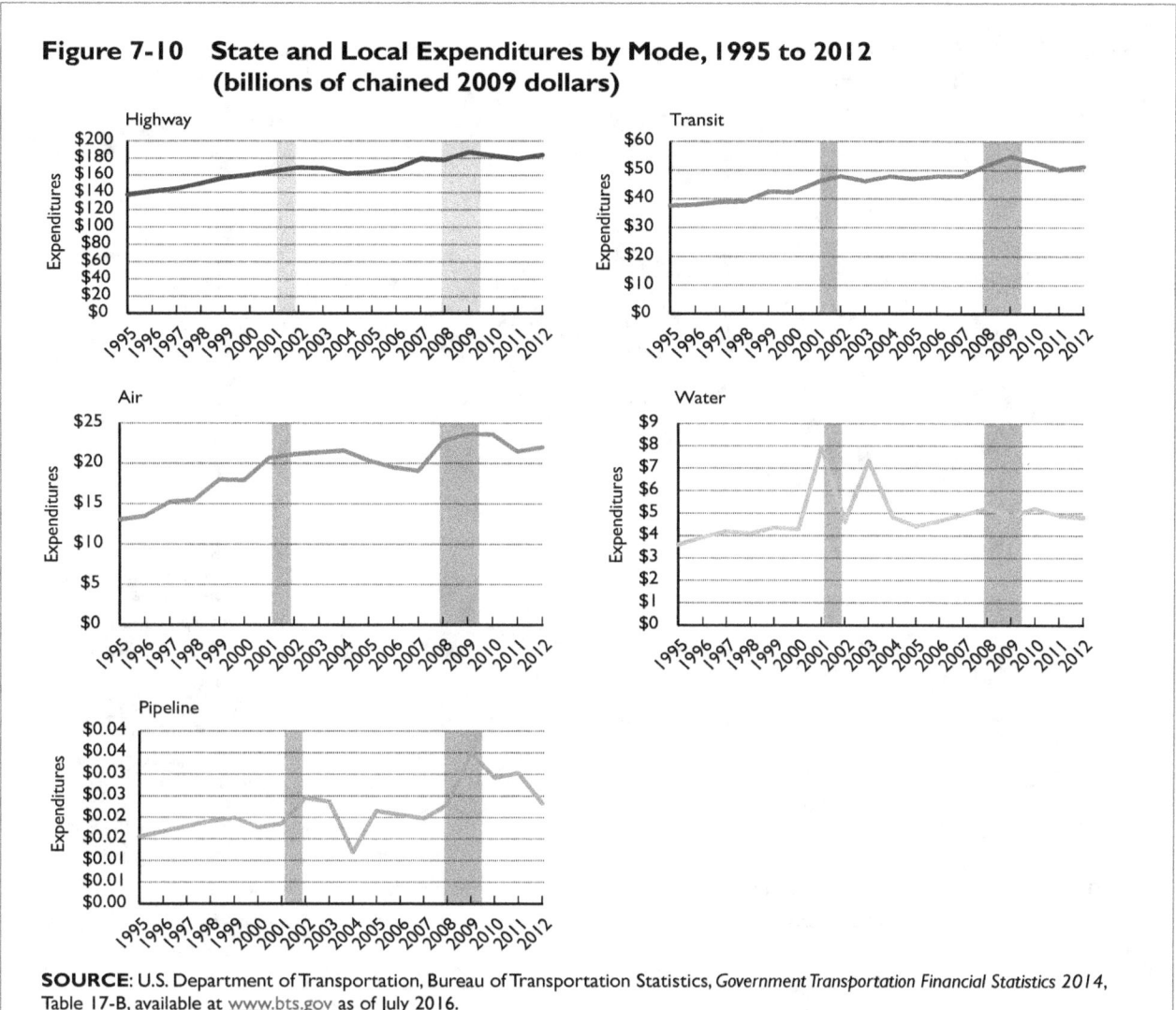

Figure 7-10 State and Local Expenditures by Mode, 1995 to 2012 (billions of chained 2009 dollars)

SOURCE: U.S. Department of Transportation, Bureau of Transportation Statistics, *Government Transportation Financial Statistics 2014*, Table 17-B, available at www.bts.gov as of July 2016.

over half of their transportation expenditures to transit (81.3 and 61.4 percent, respectively) (figure 7-12). In contrast, inland low-density states in the Great Plains, like North Dakota and Kansas, spend over 90 percent of their transportation expenditures on highways. Nevada, Alaska, and Virginia spend a larger percentage of their transportation dollars (20 percent or more) on aviation. Finally, Washington, Virginia, South Carolina, and Louisiana, with economically significant ports, spend greater percentages on water transportation (6 to 9 percent) than most other states.

State and Federal Funding of Public Transit

The amount that states spend on public transit varies greatly by state, as does the relative share of state and Federal Government spending on transit (box 7-4). In 2012 New York had the highest state and federal transit expenditure ($6.17 billion), with the state government contributing 72 percent ($4.47 billion) and the Federal Government contributing 28 percent ($1.70 billion) (figure 7-13). Figure 7-13 demonstrates that a small number of states account for the majority of transit expenditures:

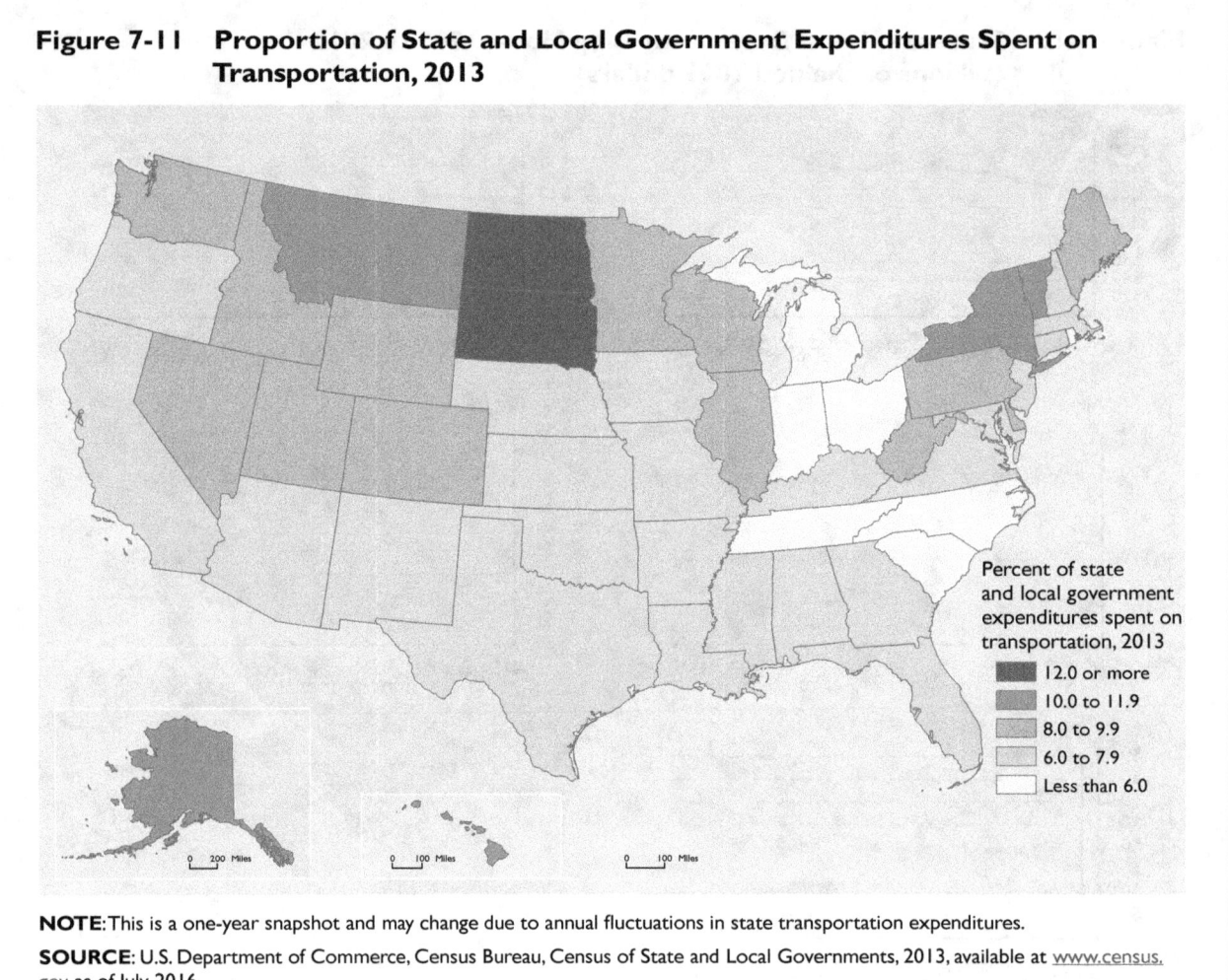

Figure 7-11   Proportion of State and Local Government Expenditures Spent on Transportation, 2013

Percent of state and local government expenditures spent on transportation, 2013

- 12.0 or more
- 10.0 to 11.9
- 8.0 to 9.9
- 6.0 to 7.9
- Less than 6.0

0   200 Miles

0   100 Miles

0   100 Miles

NOTE: This is a one-year snapshot and may change due to annual fluctuations in state transportation expenditures.

SOURCE: U.S. Department of Commerce, Census Bureau, Census of State and Local Governments, 2013, available at www.census. gov as of July 2016.

while the top states have average expenditures of $1.87 billion, the remaining states have average expenditures of $139 million. Within the top 10 states, the proportion of state spending ranges from a low of 4 percent in Texas to a high of 82 percent in Maryland. State governments in Hawaii, Arizona, Alabama, and Utah spent no money on transit in 2012.

Government Transportation Revenue v. Expenditures

Figure 7-14 illustrates combined transportation revenue and expenditures for all levels of government from 1995 to 2012 in chained

2009 dollars. Transportation revenue includes own-source revenue as well as supporting revenue from other sources like general funds. Transportation expenditures exceeded revenues from 2001 to 2004 and in 2009 and 2010. Governments increased transportation spending from 2001 to 2003 to improve security after the September 11, 2001 terrorist attacks, and the American Recovery and Reinvestment Act of 2009 increased federal supporting revenue in 2009. In addition, the recession of 2007 to 2009 suppressed consumption-based, own-source revenues, such as the motor fuel tax, as well as state and local supporting revenues.

Figure 7-12 Transportation Expenditures and Revenues by State and Local Governments, 2012 (billions of dollars)

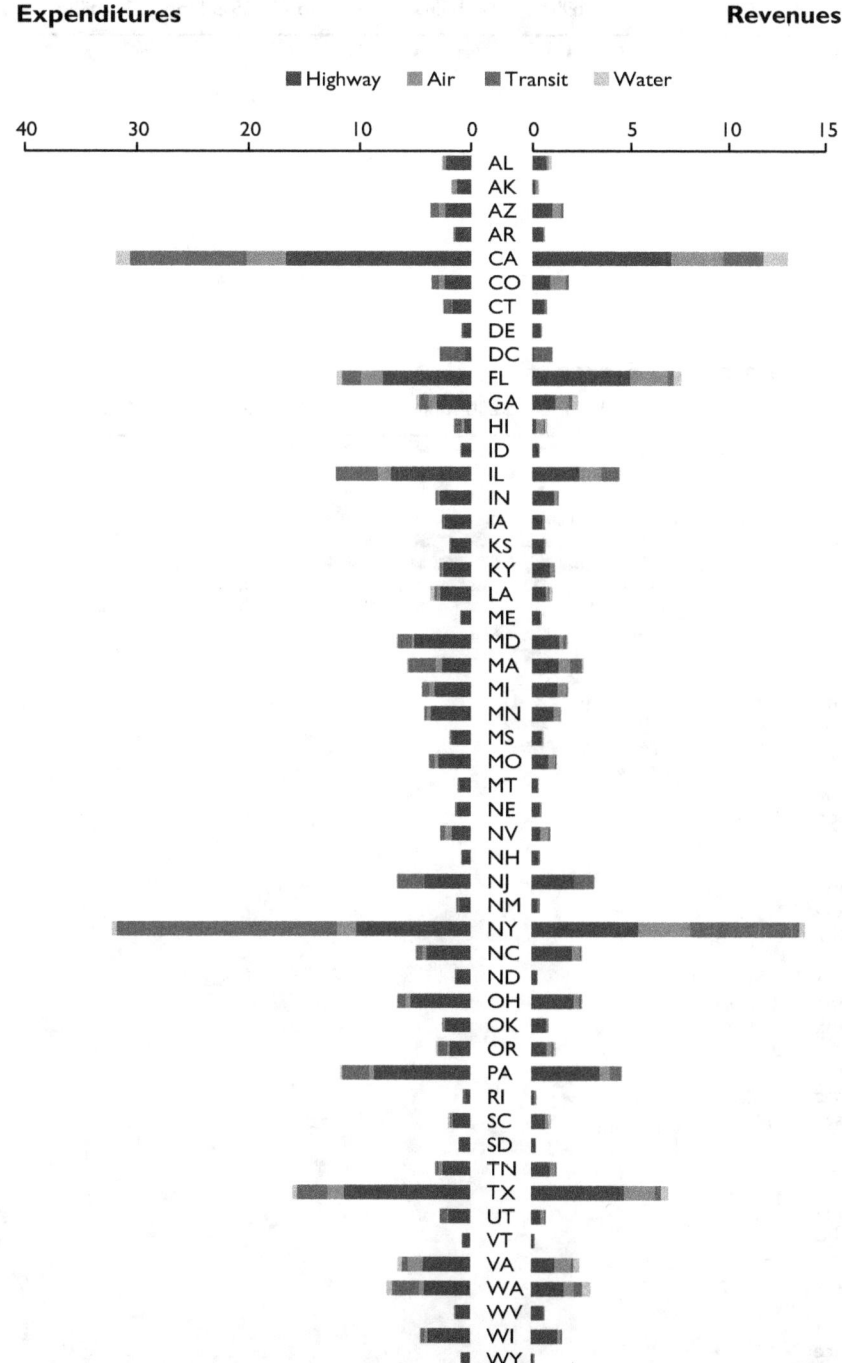

SOURCE: U.S. Department of Transportation, Bureau of Transportation Statistics, *State Transportation Statistics*, Table 6-8, available at www.bts.gov as of July 2016.

Figure 7-13 Federal and State Funding of Public Transit, 2012

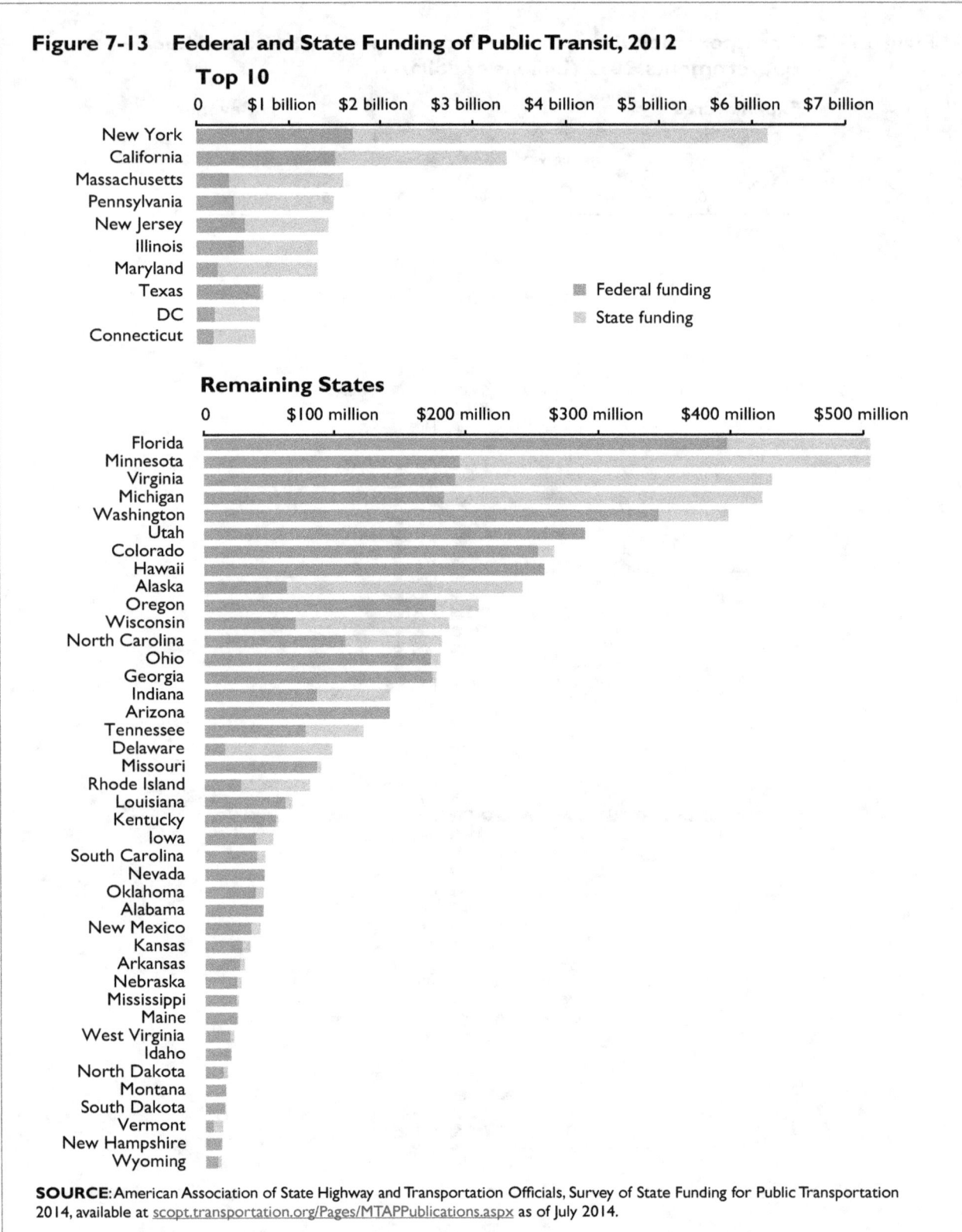

SOURCE: American Association of State Highway and Transportation Officials, Survey of State Funding for Public Transportation 2014, available at scopt.transportation.org/Pages/MTAPPublications.aspx as of July 2014.

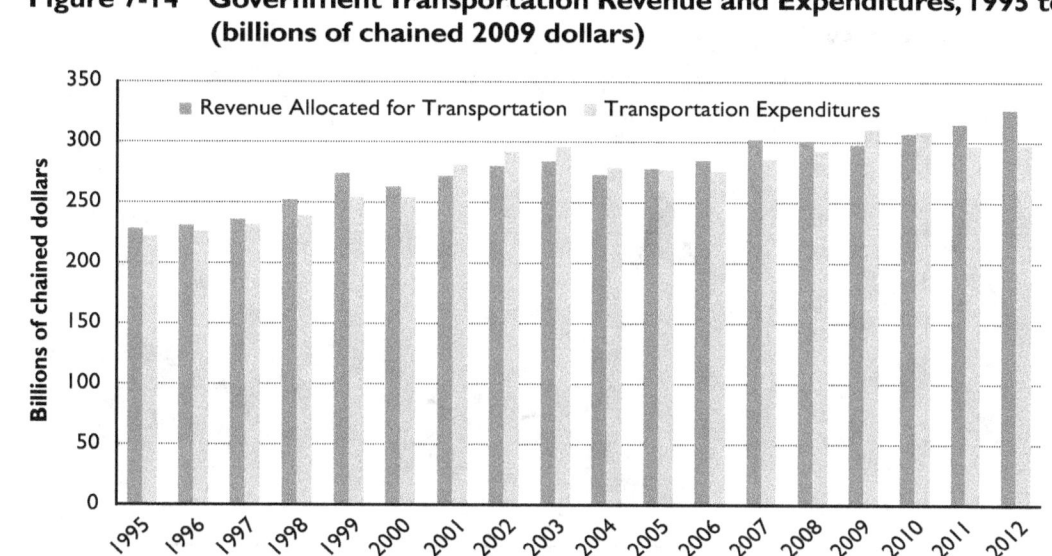

Figure 7-14 Government Transportation Revenue and Expenditures, 1995 to 2012 (billions of chained 2009 dollars)

NOTE: Revenue includes own-source revenue and supporting revenue.

SOURCE: U.S. Department of Transportation, Bureau of Transportation Statistics, *Government Transportation Financial Statistics 2014*, Table 2-B, available at www.bts.gov as of July 2016.

National Highway Cost Construction Index

Construction costs affect the amounts that governments spend on new roads, highways, and bridges. Construction costs depend on the prices of many different inputs, including materials like steel and asphalt, labor costs, and overhead costs. The *National Highway Cost Construction Index (NHCCI)* measures the prices that state transportation departments pay for

Box 7-5 National Highway Cost Construction Index

The National Highway Construction Cost Index (NHCCI), published quarterly since March 2003, uses a database of successful bids on state highway projects, which includes quotes on the specific items that comprise the projects. The database includes the costs of the material involved, the cost of labor to install it, and profit and overhead. The average price charged is calculated for each item in each state, and these price changes are then combined into a national index based on a market basket of items.

roadway construction materials and services (box 7-5). It can be used to track price changes in highway construction, plan and budget funding for infrastructure, and convert current-dollar highway construction expenditures to real (inflation-adjusted) expenditures.

In recent years, the NHCCI has shown a trend similar to the broader economy. Figure 7-15 shows that the NHCCI increased by 8.5 percent from March 2003 to December 2015. The NHCCI increased 41.8 percent between December 2003 and September 2006 when housing construction boomed and global raw material prices increased; however, this dramatic increase was followed by an equally dramatic decline of 26.1 percent from September 2006 to December 2009 when the economy went into recession from 2007 to 2009. Since December 2009, the NHCCI has shown some fluctuation while increasing 4.2 percent from December 2009 to December 2015.

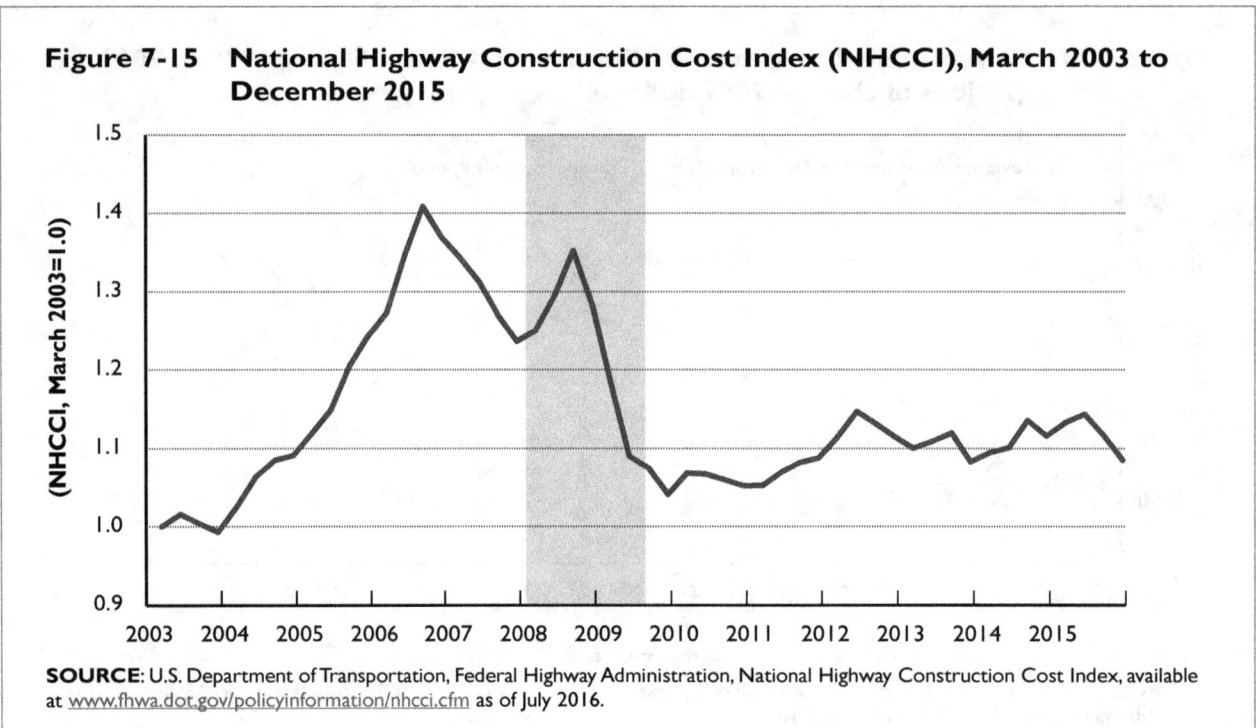

Figure 7-15   National Highway Construction Cost Index (NHCCI), March 2003 to December 2015

SOURCE: U.S. Department of Transportation, Federal Highway Administration, National Highway Construction Cost Index, available at www.fhwa.dot.gov/policyinformation/nhcci.cfm as of July 2016.

8 VALUE OF TRANSPORTATION INFRASTRUCTURE

Highways, streets, railroad lines, transit systems, ports, and other transportation infrastructure constitute one of the most important economic resources of the United States. Transportation is a capital-intensive activity, and transportation infrastructure supports the economic activities of households, transportation companies, other private firms, and governments. The infrastructure is built and owned by federal and local governments (e.g., streets, highways, airports, and transit systems), as well as by the private sector (e.g., railroads, pipelines, and support infrastructure, such as terminals).

This chapter focuses on measuring the value of infrastructure, discussing current measures of physical infrastructure as well as the more challenging measurement of the benefits that society derives from using the infrastructure. The physical measures of transportation infrastructure include *Value of Transportation Capital Stock*, produced by the Bureau of Economic Analysis (BEA); and *Value of Construction Put in Place*, produced by the Census Bureau. These measures estimate the value of transportation infrastructure in terms of the resources used to construct and maintain it. Estimating the value of transportation infrastructure in terms of the mobility it provides to businesses and individuals, however, is more difficult and is the subject of study by a Transportation Research Board (TRB) task force.

Value of Transportation Capital Stock for Infrastructure

BEA measures the value of transportation infrastructure by estimating the value of the Nation's transportation capital stock (box 8-1). As of 2014 the Nation's capital stock for transportation infrastructure has an

---

Box 8-1 Capital Stock

Capital stock refers to the capital in existence on a certain date. To be classified as capital, an asset must be durable and expected to remain in service for at least one year. Assets expected to remain in service for less than a year are categorized as *consumption goods*. Capital stock for transportation infrastructure includes fixed structures such as railroad tracks, airports, transit stations, bus shelters, and locks and dams.

SOURCE: U.S. Department of Transportation, Bureau of Transportation Statistics, 2016.

---

estimated value of $5.31 trillion (figure 8-1).[1] BEA's estimates use a weighted average of expenditures to expand capacity (by building new infrastructure) and expenditures to maintain, repair, and replace existing infrastructure, minus estimated depreciation. The depreciation estimates assume that a fixed percentage of the stock depreciates each year. These estimates are done separately for different assets such as roadways, bridges, railroad tracks, waterway locks, and other fixed network assets. Transportation rolling stock, such as locomotives, automobiles, buses, and boats, is not included in BEA's estimates of the capital stock. The estimates also do not include the value of land where the infrastructure is placed.

Figure 8-1 shows public and private transportation capital stock by mode. Federal, state, and local governments own 76 percent of the Nation's transportation capital stock by value, with an estimated value of $4.07 trillion in 2014. Highways and streets, which account for 83 percent of that value ($3.37 trillion), serve many users and modes—passenger vehicles, freight and service trucks, transit buses, pedestrians,

---

[1] Other categories of transportation capital stock include personal vehicles and parts, in-house transportation, and commercial truck transportation. In 2014, the nation's transportation capital stock has an estimated value of $8.06 trillion.

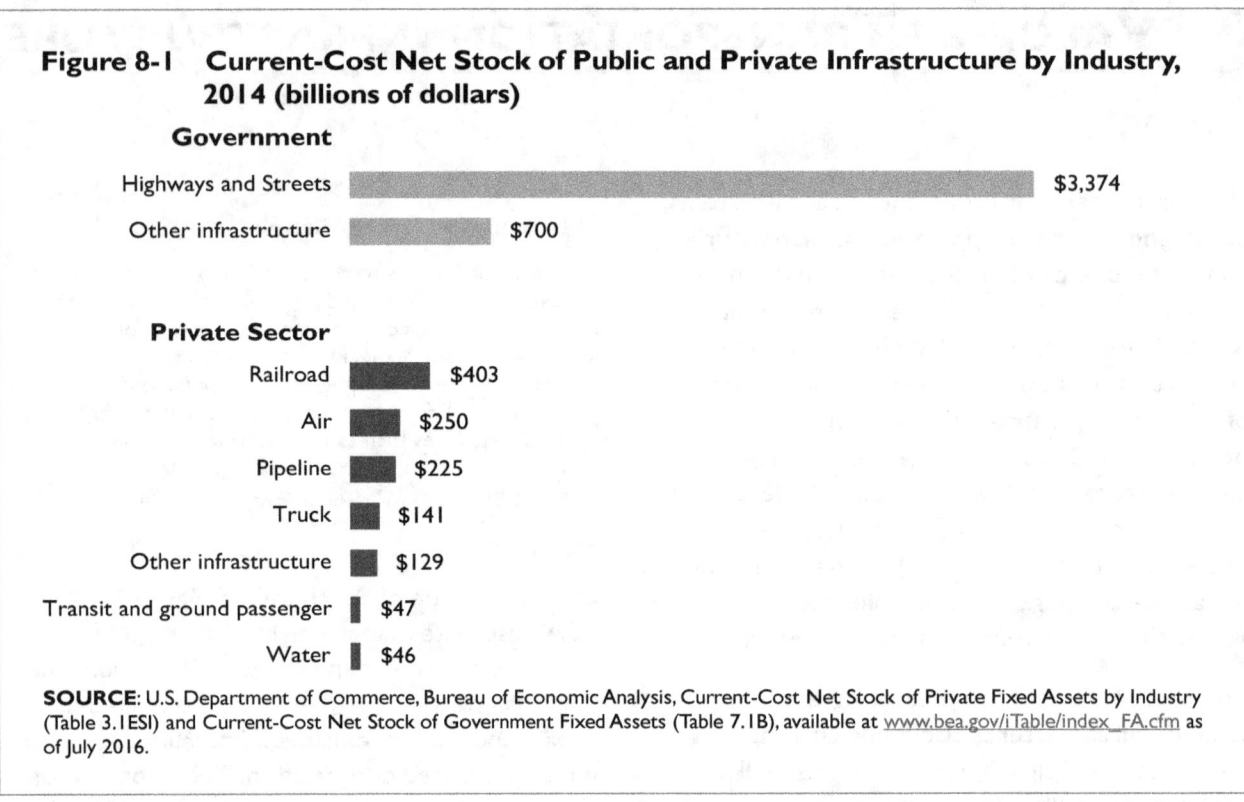

Figure 8-1   Current-Cost Net Stock of Public and Private Infrastructure by Industry, 2014 (billions of dollars)

Government

Highways and Streets — $3,374

Other infrastructure — $700

Private Sector

Railroad — $403

Air — $250

Pipeline — $225

Truck — $141

Other infrastructure — $129

Transit and ground passenger — $47

Water — $46

SOURCE: U.S. Department of Commerce, Bureau of Economic Analysis, Current-Cost Net Stock of Private Fixed Assets by Industry (Table 3.1ESI) and Current-Cost Net Stock of Government Fixed Assets (Table 7.1B), available at www.bea.gov/iTable/index_FA.cfm as of July 2016.

and cyclists. Governments also own other transportation infrastructure such as transit systems and airports, with an estimated value of $700 billion.

The private sector owns the remaining 24 percent of transportation infrastructure, with an estimated value of $1.24 trillion in 2014. The largest amount ($403 billion) is owned by the railroad companies, which own, maintain, and operate their own tracks, railroad yards, and associated facilities. Pipeline companies also own and operate their own infrastructure ($225 billion). Finally, the transportation companies that use public infrastructure, such as trucking companies and airlines, own support infrastructure such as maintenance facilities, warehouses, and other buildings.

Value of Construction Put in Place

The Value of Construction Put in Place survey program, administered by the U.S. Census

Bureau, provides monthly estimates of the value of construction work done in the United States. These estimates cover new structures and improvements to existing structures in the private and public sectors, and are used by the BEA to measure the current value of capital stock for infrastructure. Construction costs include labor, materials, equipment rental, architectural and engineering work, overhead, interest and taxes, contractor profits, and miscellaneous overhead and office charges.

In 2015 private and public spending on transportation construction totaled $134 billion (figure 8-2). Public transportation construction accounted for 90 percent of that amount ($121 billion), and private transportation construction accounted for the remaining 10 percent ($13.2 billion). Highway and street construction accounted for 74 percent of public spending on transportation construction ($89.6 billion), and construction for air, land, and water transportation facilities accounted for the

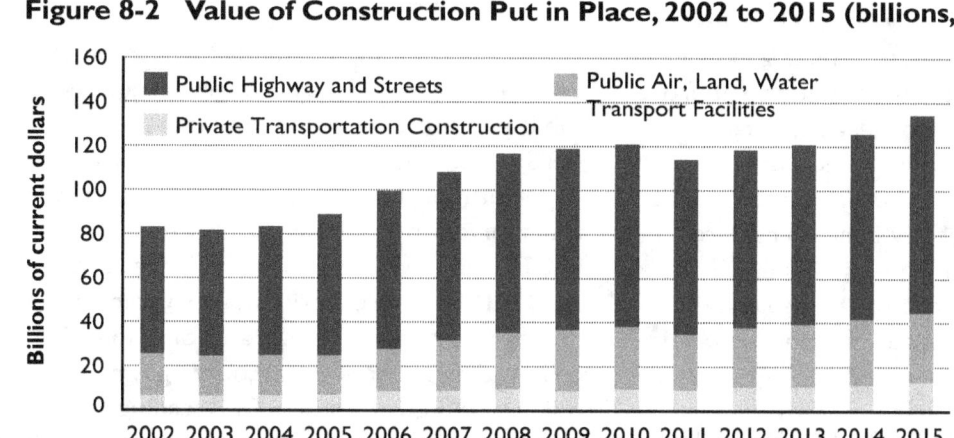

Figure 8-2 Value of Construction Put in Place, 2002 to 2015 (billions, current dollars)

- Public Highway and Streets
- Public Air, Land, Water Transport Facilities
- Private Transportation Construction

SOURCE: U.S. Department of Commerce, Census Bureau, Construction Spending Survey, available at www.census.gov/construction/ c30/c30index.html as of July 2016.

remaining 26 percent ($31.5 billion). Although the amount and composition of construction varies from year to year, the value of transportation construction put in place has increased an average of 4 percent per year since 2002, dropping slightly in 2011 but increasing to a peak in 2015.

Estimating the Benefits of Transportation Infrastructure

The previous two approaches are useful for understanding what it costs to construct and maintain transportation infrastructure, but they do not reveal the value that the infrastructure provides to society. For example, it may cost $100 million to construct a new bridge, but the *value* of the bridge comes from the benefits which result from connecting businesses and individuals to jobs, markets, and social functions. Two approaches are typically taken to estimate the benefits that society derives from using transportation infrastructure. One approach is bottom-up from the project level (a microeconomic approach); the other is top-down from the national account level (a macroeconomic approach).

In theory, the two approaches should yield similar estimates, but the approaches do not completely overlap. Project-level analysis potentially understates the effects that a project will have on the national economy. For example, a new interchange near an international port may attract additional international trade, creating national economic benefits beyond the project zone. At the same time, however, the project-level analysis will include freight shipments which shift from other U.S. ports to the upgraded port facility and therefore have no net effect on the national economy. Both sets of shipments would need to be measured accurately to estimate the national economic benefits of the interchange.

The macroeconomic approach, in contrast, uses the BEA's National Income and Product Accounts (NIPA), which provide aggregate measures of the Nation's economic output at the national, regional, and industry levels. Econometric analysis links project-level effects to changes in GDP or changes in the value of capital stock. However, the analysis is complicated and measures only large transportation investments, such as the Interstate Highway System.

93

Accessibility Benefits

The government and the private sector invest in building new infrastructure, maintaining existing infrastructure, and expanding capacity to improve connectivity and address congestion. These investments provide individuals and businesses access to jobs, markets, and other opportunities. Measuring these accessibility benefits requires another approach to estimate the benefits of transportation infrastructure and evaluate whether transportation systems meet the needs of residents.

More research is necessary to quantify and link transportation accessibility to wages, consumer prices, and the well-being of individuals. The Texas Transportation Institute, Federal Aviation Administration, and others have made advances to estimate the *cost* of reduced accessibility from travel delays, but individuals also receive *benefits* when they reach their destination. Data sources, like the National Household Travel Survey, the American Community Survey, and the Longitudinal Employer-Household Dynamics, allow researchers to measure these benefits by matching household locations to the locations of employment, consumer markets, and social connections.

Task Force on Value of Transportation Infrastructure

In MAP-21 (Moving Ahead for Progress in the 21st Century Act, 2012), Congress required the Bureau of Transportation Statistics (BTS) to provide "a national accounting of expenditures and capital stocks on each mode of transportation and intermodal combination." In FAST (Fixing America's Surface Transportation Act, 2015), Congress continued to voice interest in measuring the value of transportation. To ensure that the national accounting is robust, reliable, and up-to-date, BTS is leading a 3-year research effort to develop new data and methods to quantify the value of transportation to the economy. BTS funded the TRB's Task Force on Value of Transportation Infrastructure (AB020T), which includes leading experts on economics and transportation infrastructure from industry, academia, and state and federal governments, to conduct the research. In 2014 the task force hosted a workshop to review existing methods to estimate the value of transportation infrastructure and its role in the economy.[2] The task force continues to extend existing methods and develop new methods to allow BTS to provide more meaningful statistics for decision makers.

---

[2] http://onlinepubs.trb.org/onlinepubs/circulars/ec192.pdf

www.ingramcontent.com/pod-product-compliance
Lightning Source LLC
Chambersburg PA
CBHW081607220526
45468CB00010B/2798